Straight from the Lip

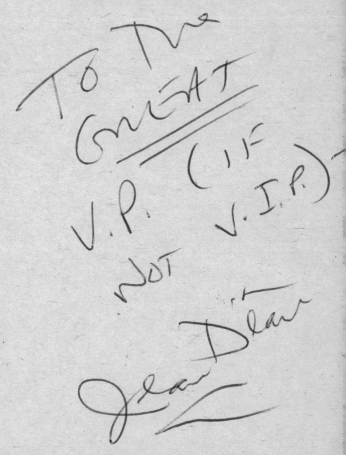

To The
GREAT
V.P. (IF
V.I.P.)
NOT
Jean Dlau

Straight
FROM THE
LIP

BY JEAN DÊAU

General
— PAPERBACKS —
Toronto, Canada

Published by arrangement with Fitzhenry and Whiteside Ltd.

Published in 1987 by General Publishing Paperbacks

ISBN 0-7736-7129-3

Cover illustration: Graham Pilsworth
Cover design: Brant Cowie/Artplus

Printed in Canada

For Jean Chrétien
Don Johnston
Gérard Pelletier
Who Showed Us The Way.

Introduction by

JEAN CHRÉTIEN

I was asked by the publishers of this anthology of Canadian political autobiographies for some words about my career, and what has happened to me since I wrote my wildly successful story, *Straight From the Heart*.

Are they crazy? Do they honestly think that I'd risk undercutting the sales of the new paperback edition of my book? Do they really think that I'd tell the *truth* about why I had to leave politics, because of the dirty, double-crossing dealings of Ol' Blue Eyes? Do they honestly think that I would help out a stupid collection of (probably fictional) autobiographies of Great Canadians, when I'm making big bucks from plugging my own?

No way. If you want to read my self-censored thoughts about Turner's incompetent attempts to "unite" the great Liberal party which he so disastrously disunited, then pick up the paperback version of my book, available from Bantam-Seal ($4.95). I don't *have* to be obsequious and politically-sweet anymore; I'm out of that racket. And as the dozens of fools you've probably included in your rip-off of my book will no doubt prove, it's a racket which few Good Guys like me have ever lowered themselves to belong to.

JACQUES HÉBERT

"When I was a child, I spake as a child, I understood as a child, I thought as a child. But when I became a man, I put away childish things."

1 Corinthians 13:11

I always liked that first line, but never the second. As I learned from Pierre on our trip to China in 1960, temper tantrums can often be successful. Holding your breath is alright; jumping up and down is good too. But refusing to eat any food and threatening to starve yourself to death can work wonders!

Straight from the Chin

BRIAN MULRONEY

(Dictated simultaneously in both French and English, on the Ontario/Quebec border, with eyes firmly facing south, to our Good Friends, the United States)

Here it is, barely two full years into my Prime Ministership, and things have been going so well for me, for my party, and for Canada, that it behooves me to jot down a few words for this anthology of Canadian political autobiographies. We've made a few mistakes, sure — well, my cabinet ministers have, but there is no question that our excellence is being proven daily, and that our direction is a firm and steady one: toward the United States.

It was during those years of my youth, when my mind was being honed, my future developed, and my chin sculpted, that I became interested in politics. I considered the Liberals briefly, but quickly realized that they ran a closed shop, and had no place for a boy like me.

I was impressed by Bob Stanfield, then the leader of Nova Scotia's Tory opposition, and, with a feeling of pride and eagerness, became a Progressive Conservative: my heart beating wildly, my feet anxious to run, my eyes firmly fixed on the main chance. In 1956, I was a youth delegate at the PC convention in Ottawa that chose Dief as its national leader. I then became the national VP of Youth for Diefenbaker, and made sure that every national leader in the country, even the Chief himself, knew who I was. If you think the CBC is a network, you don't know what networking is until you've studied my career.

It's been the fast track ever since: upon the recommendation of my good law-school buddy Michel Cogger — who is in the Senate now — I joined the prestigious Montreal firm of Ogilvy, Cope, Porteous, Montgomery, Renault, Clarke, and Kirkpatrick. It irritated me that the name Clarke was in the firm's name, and that the name Mulroney was not, but I was just an articling law student, so I guess I had to bide my time and wait. I was hardly sitting around. I had such clients as the Power Corporation — whose head, Paul Desmarais, later helped bankroll my 1976 campaign — and Iron Ore of Canada, which I later served as its president. Such are the ways of bright young baritones from Baie Comeau.

My tens of millions of admirers across North America, and now the Far East, will find this hard to believe, but I was relatively unknown nationally, until 1974. That was when the workers went on a rampage at the James Bay project, and I was appointed to a Royal Commission of Inquiry into Union Freedom. It was headed by Robert Cliche, and I have been speaking in clichés ever since.

It was an exciting time! I was on TV! I received thousands of inches of newspaper columns! I couldn't have had my name used any more, had I changed it to Brian La Presse. So what else could I do, but run for the leadership of the federal Progressive Conservative Party, in 1976? I had all the qualifications: a big chin. A big bankroll. A beautiful, ethnic wife. And the greatest attraction of all: I had never served in public office before, so I had no shameful past to cover up. Not like my good friend Claude Wagner, whose secret trust fund I had nothing whatsoever to do with setting up, nor had I anything to do with leaking the story of the fund during the leadership convention. It was my other good buddy from Laval, Peter White, and I have no idea why he did a thing like that.

I did astonishingly well, coming in second, on the first ballot, behind the pre-convention favourite, Claude Wagner. After four ballots, it was over. I had lost, for the first time in my fairy-tale rise to the top. I don't recall who won, but it's not important; I'm the Prime Minister now.

I had to find employment once more. And soon after the leadership campaign, my good friend William Bennett offered me the post of executive VP for corporate affairs in the Iron Ore Company of Canada, and I became IOC's president a year later.

As with everything I've touched in my life — you too, Mila — it turned to gold. I made the firm a success. I ended its labour problems and began to turn a profit. True, I had to kill Schefferville, but as a great American general once said, while fighting in Viet Nam, "sometimes you have to destroy a town in order to save it."

And, you see, I really couldn't lose. Even when Iron Ore closed down the Schefferville operation, I offered a generous settlement to the workers, proving my unbeatable mixture of realism and compassion. That's really what politics are all about, so inevitably the P.C.s chose me when poor Joe Clark found himself being forced to hold a leadership review.

What could I do? Joe had been so successful, winning the Prime Ministership back in 1979, and managing to stay in power for nine long months, that it was difficult to criticize the guy. True, my good friend Jean-Yves Lortie had worked to undermine good old Joe in Winnipeg, but I certainly had nothing whatsoever to do with that. The people were crying out for a bilingual Quebecois Irish Catholic handsome debonaire leader with a wife of the same name, and I've never been one to not answer a call. I won on the fourth ballot, and the rest is history.

A great history it is, too: My winning the by-election in Central Nova, out in the Maritimes. My magnificent debates and attacks in the House of Commons as the leader of the Official Opposition. My incredible victory in September, 1984, when I kicked Grit ass right across the country, and took back the province of Quebec as a Tory stronghold.

In the past twenty-four months, I've given the Canadian people what they voted for: Support of NATO. Support of the invasion of Grenada. Support of the cruise missile testing. Non-support of the USSR. A refusal to give puffy patronage jobs to unworthy Grits. And most important, an open hand and open pant pockets to our Best Friends on Earth, the Americans.

Where would we be without the Americans? Who provides us with a nuclear umbrella? Who gives us all the TV and movies that we love so much? Who has taken such good care of all our mines, oil wells, gold, silver, transportation, factories, and everything else that they've bought up, over the years? God, I love the Americans! I'm so crazy about the Yanks, I wept when the Toronto Blue Jays eliminated the team in the second-last game of 1985.

I've surrounded myself with the best friends, buddies and cronies that a man can have, and they are helping me to make North America great again.

Sarajevo, Dublin, Montreal, Ottawa and Washington, D.C. will unite in embrace, through Mila, myself, my great legal career, my wonderful political career, and my dear friend "Irish" Ronnie Reagan. Let cabinet ministers fall as they may, let shingles shake down from the heavens, let the Canadian book industry tear its

12

pages out — who buys books anyway? *I* never do! It's Irish charm that the people want, and they've got it as long as they show the intelligence to re-elect it. I want you all to please join me now in the singing of The Star-Spang. . . I mean O Canada. And don't forget, with me around it'll be hard not to think of the Baie!

DALTON CAMP

Dearest Brian,

Calm down. *Calm down.* I've got *everything* under *control.* Forget about Roch, ignore Bissonette, get your mind off Wolf, stop thinking about Bazin, dump Doucet doldrums.

None of it is *important*, Brian! It'll all *pass!* And after what I did to Dief, the party wouldn't *dare* do it to you; we Tories have too rotten a reputation for killing our Messengers to let ourselves murder *you.* (You can partly thank what you did to Joe for this attitude as well, Brian. Waytogo!)

You'll bounce back, I *promise* you. Whatever goes down must come up, Brian — it's a scientific fact. Or is it what goes up must go down? Anyway, every dog has its day, Brian, and you've got admit the last few hundred days have been a *bitch.*

Here's what you do: Stonewall. Keep travelling. Keep throwing money at the public. Try to cut down the patronage at least 5-10% from the present rate. And take a few more trips to Africa; at least the blacks love ya.

Hell, you can even leave your autobiography in this book, *Straight From the Lip,* just as optimistic as it was from the first edition back in the summer of 1986. After all, what has changed? I *promised* you that I wouldn't let you peak too soon before the next election, and I've certainly come through, haven't I?

And remember what I keep telling you every day, Bri: If I could sell cigarettes for a quarter-century, and convince millions of Canadians that they were good for them, I can sure as hell sell them on the federal PCs. And even on you.

> Yours forever, as I used to write Dief,
>
> Dalton

PAT CARNEY

If you want it done, let a woman do it. That's what I say. And if any woman is big enough to do the job, it's me, Pat Carney, the first woman to ever hold the portfolio of Minister of Energy, Mines and Resources, and the first economist to do it, too. And then, I bounced over to the International Trade portfolio — and if anyone knows how to bounce, it's me. This girl knows what she's doing, and if the boys don't, they'd better watch their asses.

Other politicians just *talk* big about having been around. But what guy or gal has been around as much as *me*? I was born in Shanghai in 1935 — I had a womb mate, James — to a Canadian civil servant father and a South African journalist mom. I was profoundly influenced by both: I became a very fine journalist, just like my mother, and I've been shanghaied into more writing and political assignments than you can shake a Grit at.

We returned to Canada, right before the Japanese entered Shanghai, just in time to see the Canadian government make the Japanese-Canadians leave British Columbia. There is an amazing symmetry in this world, if you are open to it.

My daddy got a degree in Guelph, Ontario, and then worked as a government vet out in B.C., where my brother and I went to school. We attended the University of British Columbia, and both worked on the campus paper, the *Ubyssey*, and did some writing for the Vancouver *Province*, on the side. My buddies back then were Joe Schlesinger, Alexander Ross and Allan Fotheringham, and look where I am today, and where *those* guys are: Still slugging it out in the lousy fields of electronic and print journalism. It's just as they say: Girls mature faster than boys. Although you would *think* that they'd eventually catch up, wouldn't you?

By 1955, I joined the staff of the *Province*, and married a newspaperman the following year. We had a son, and were divorced by 1969. But in the meantime, the important things: I became a major business journalist, jumped over to the *Vancouver Sun*, and became just one of the boys in the Ottawa Parliamentary Press Gallery in 1968, hopping back and forth across the country like a bunny in heat.

15

It was a great time to be alive, a woman, a journalist, and a business writer: free gifts, free rides, free favours, freebies galore! Of course, as Brian Mulroney, Michael Wilson and I have often cautioned Canadians, there is no free lunch anymore. But this was back in the '60s and '70s, when the times were still good.

I've always been a firm believer in conflict of interest. It leads to exciting possibilities and great potential for economic reward. So I jumped up to Yellowknife, got hired to write a puffy book about the 1970 royal visit to the North, and set up a consulting company to help plug for Northern development. It was all marvelous experience for a future career in politics: Running roughshod over Indian and native lifestyles, ignoring social costs of pipeline development, and forgetting about the environment. I have managed to preserve these attitudes, and have brought them into the Mulroney government.

What it comes down to is, I realized that all Northern development is positive, and that's that. Ahh, if only Life was as clear and straightforward.

Throughout the 1970s, my career continued to make great leaps forward, which is a famous economic term, by the way. I was a member of the Economic Council of Canada from 1974 to 1978; a press officer for the United Nations Habitat Conference in Vancouver in 1976; and then decided to run against Art Phillips in the 1979 election in Vancouver Centre, even though he had a pretty wife to support him, and I did not.

I won, I'll have you know. I won. It was by only two votes, but I won. I should mention, in passing, that there was a recount, and I lost by 95 votes, but these things happen in politics, and should be ultimately ignored.

My good friend Joe Clark, who was then the Prime Minister of Canada for that hectic, exciting nine months, named me to a number of important committees, and urged me to run again. So I did, beating the pants off my opponent in the 1980 election, even as the country turned tragically and foolishly back to Trudeau. Joe Clark remained my warm supporter, and he made me the Tory critic for Secretary of State from 1980 to 1981, and the critic of Finance from 1981 to 1982. Having been used to working in the shadows — the nights in Yellowknife are very, very long — I made a great shadow minister.

16

Then, as is well known, good old Joe had some problems in the early 1980s, trying to keep his fellow Tories from digging in the knife. Joe had expected me to be a passionate supporter, but I personally save my passion for oil companies, oil exploration, Northern development, and, since the summer of 1986, for Free Trade. I was the co-chairperson of both those conventions in 1983, and I decided to keep a very neutral position. As Barry Goldwater once said, ''Extremism in pursuit of neutrality is no problem.'' Or something like that.

Joe felt betrayed, I must admit, but then, he usually feels betrayed about almost everything. And he's usually right. But neutrality has its own reward, as I like to say; I was rewarded with the post of Energy critic in the shadow cabinet of Brian. And I've already told you how well I work in the shadows, haven't I?

There are great advantages to being a woman in what has traditionally been a male-dominated field. For instance, the time I was refused entry to the Calgary Petroleum Club, whose members apparently suffer from fear of women, I merely grinned and sluffed it off. After all, it is certainly a serious phobia, and I hope that most of the men get over it. Because I plan to kick some ass the next time I'm in that two-bit oil town.

My beliefs are simple, and can be clearly stated: Oil is the greatest thing since sliced bread. The Arctic pipeline is the greatest thing since oil. Oil prices should, and probably will, hover in the $30 to $40 a barrel range for the foreseeable future, or I plan to personally and physically maim each and every member of OPEC, individually. And I can do it, too. I'm no featherweight, you know. Anyway, that's all in the past; I don't have to check oil prices anymore. I've now got my hands full with Simon Reisman, a man who could give Mother Teresa ulcers. But then, replacing James Kelleher as salesman of our federal government's free-trade policies was as tough as Winston Churchill filling the shoes of Neville Chamberlain. In other words, not too tough at all.

I am consistent, that's for sure. For most of my life, I believed that oil companies could do no wrong. Brian might screw up, occasionally; Joe, nearly every other day. But the oil companies? They wanted only the best for Canada and for all Canadians. I hadn't forgotten all those great trips and gifts. And nowadays, I believe that Free Trade is Good for Canada. It's as simple as that. *Oh, shut up, Hurtig. Just shut up already.*

I am Woman. I am Westerner. I am Free Trade. Sure, I'm number 2 to Joe Clark, which is something even his wife won't agree to. But how can I fail? As dear Brian said back in July of 1986, "Now, you watch Pat Carney go. She's got the ball and you just watch her run." God, imagine how well I could do in this cabinet if I had two of them.

And as for the 1990s? Just fill in the blank in this puzzle: Golda Meir. Indira Gandhi. Margaret Thatcher. Corazon Aquino. _____.

I'll give you a hint: She sits just behind Mulroney during Question Period.

Congratulations. Go to the head of the class.

Straight from Yasser, That's My Baby

MARCEL PRUD'HOMME

It's a real thrill to be the newly elected chairman of the Liberal caucus, especially over that shrill pill, Copps. And as for my passion for the Arab cause, what's so improper about that? We Canadians have *always* felt more strongly about oil than principles.

And what should we put in our cars, anyway?

Chicken soup???

GERALD BOUEY

Wayne Gretzky's not the *only* small-town boy who's out to break records. Look what happened during *my* tenure as Canada's Governor of the Bank of Canada in the IML (International Money League).

I presided over the *first* Canadian bank failures in 62 years!

I reigned during the *worst* recession in 40 years!

When I tried to dry up the money supply, the interest rates topped 22% — *the highest ever*!

So what do I get for breaking all these fabulous records?

Nothing but heartache and bellyaching. There's Canadians for you.

So I'm stepping down. Let's see what you think of the Crow rates.

SHEILA COPPS

Any Tories who are reading my autobiography now had better listen, and listen well: I'm not taking any crap from anybody, especially you Neanderthal Conservatives. (My apologies to any Neanderthals who may be reading this.) And as far as Chub-Chub Crosbie's referring to me as a titmouse, lemme tell him, he's only half-right.

All right, so what do you wanna know? How I became the lead singer in the new Canada-wide rock-throwing group, "Sheila and the Rats"? How a rookie MP from a small Ontario town like Hamilton could become the best-loved gal on the hit TV show, Question Period?

To be frank — and some say I'd make a better Frank than a Sheila — it was in my blood. My dad, Vic Copps, was the mayor of Hamilton, and my mom is a citizenship judge.

I was born in late November, 1952 — this lady ain't afraid to tell *her* age — the second of four children. When I was 8 years old, my dad ran for city controller in Hamilton, and I was his campaign manager. I had recently been kicked out of the Brownies for wearing jeans and chains to meetings, so I was ready for anything.

But what I wasn't ready for was falling in love with Pierre Trudeau. When I saw him at that leadership convention in 1968 — I was 15 and vulnerable, that I'll admit — I was a goner. Sure, Turner was cute, but Trudeau was something else! So I began to work for John Munro in the federal election of that summer, building up a great reputation in Hamilton East, which I now represent, as the world knows and as every Tory fears.

I bounced around for the next decade, not doing too much. I studied French and English at Western, worked for the Ottawa Citizen, married and divorced a reporter in less than a year, worked for *The Hamilton Spectator*, and then was asked by my beloved provincial party to run in the riding of Hamilton Centre.

It was a great honour, sort of. The riding hadn't gone Grit since the Great Depression, there was less than a month left to the campaign, and I was all of 24 years of age. But I did it. I ran for the office. And although I lost, it was by a mere 14 votes, and the political bug had bitten. (I hear there's a shot for it, but I'm waiting until it's been tried on other laboratory animals. They don't call us the Rat Pack for nothing.)

I junked journalism and went to work for Stuart Smith, the provincial party leader at that time, still slogging it out in the wilderness. And I learned how to do it right: In the 1981 election, I won Hamilton Centre by nearly 3,000 votes.

It was a real joy, being the only woman in the Ontario provincial Liberal caucus. Clod Bennett applauded me on being better looking than my party's previous MPP of the female persuasion, Margaret Campbell, who had retired at the age of 69. Another Tory MPP, Mickey (Piggy) Hennessy told me to "go back to the kitchen." How *could* I? I'd never been in a kitchen in my life.

I soon became known as a Red Grit, slightly to the left of Mao and Che. I fought passionately for a constitutional amendment to make French an official language in Ontario (they can vote); for the inclusion of homosexual rights in the Ontario Human Rights Code (they can vote too!); for equal pay for work of equal value and premium-free medicare.

Within a year, there was a widespread call for me to run for the leadership of the provincial Liberal party. I felt that the Ontario Liberals had become stultified, fossilized and petrified. No wonder they needed someone with a softer body to get them back in power, after nearly four decades of drifting. Talk about new blood: I was 29.

OK, OK, so I lost. So big deal. I'm a gambler and I'm a believer, and opportunities don't always knock twice. I ran second to David Peterson, who, I'll have you know, became Premier, just a few years after he beat me. I worked on John Munro's federal Liberal leadership campaign in the summer of 1984, and urged him to support Chrétien over Turner. So much for backing winners. But then Keith Davey and Marc Lalonde begged me to run federally, and how could I refuse? I just love it when men get on their hands and knees and beg me to do something.

So I ran, with Ol' Blue Eyes as our leader, walloping the Tories by winning a hearty 40 seats, vs. their 211. It was a tough fight, but it helped that I spoke our country's other official language (Italian). And my left-wing politics appealed to the citizens of Hamilton East, who are so unionized, they think Bob White is the official bird of Canada. I won a great majority, and joined 26 other women in that quasi-masculine club in Ottawa.

And so it has gone, since September, 1984. I have become widely admired for my tremendous pluck at Question Period, during which many of the Tories have been heard screaming, "Get the pluck out of here!"

My voice has become a source of pleasure to every Grit, and a source of dread to every Tory. It has been compared to a Starfighter crashing in West Germany, a Newfoundland foghorn, and the last cry of the seagull that Dave Winfield hit with the baseball in that famous Yankees-Blue Jays game. But Mulroney should talk! His voice sounds like a deepsea diver suffering from bends, and that little wifey of his has set back women's rights three centuries.

Anyway, we can't all lie low and act like statespersons. I have an obligation to go on search-and-destroy missions; the Good Lord, in Her Infinite Wisdom, placed me on Earth in order to make life impossible for Conservatives, and I am not about to shirk my obligations.

I recently remarried, in the summer of 1985, a guy I met in a bar, down in Florida. He had no idea what the hell an MP was, so I just knew that he was the type for me. He'll work as a TV editor in Ottawa, and it'll be nice to have a piping-hot dinner waiting for me when I come home. Would I want children? Sure, just so long as when they grow up, they don't marry Tories.

There's talk of me becoming the next head of the Liberals, but it's a bit early to think about that; hell, I'm still in my early 30s. Then again, Jean Chrétien did quit. And if Turner doesn't get his act together. . . .

Look, anything is possible for a girl from Hamilton, Ontario. I'm the Head of the Rat Pack. I drive the Tories batty. And there ain't *nobody* that's going to shush *me* up. Has Mulroney the Phony ever had *his* picture taken on a motorcycle, on the front cover of *Saturday Night*?

The first three letters of my last name are C-O-P. And the first three letters of my first name are S-H-E. And don't anybody ever forget it.

ANDRÉ BISSONNETTE
(and Hume Publishing)

THINK LIKE A MILLIONAIRE
AND YOU CAN *LIVE* LIKE A MILLIONAIRE!!!

That's right! Imagine investing with someone else's money!!

Watching your investment multiply as property values continue to rise!

And then pay the minimum tax on your profit because the government treats your investment in a favourable way!!

I, personally, made big bucks in real estate, and *you can too*!! Bissonnette's the name and real estate's the game! Would you like to win, just like I did? Read on!

Look how *moi*, a minor Canadian politician making less than $75,000 a year, copped a fortune almost overnight, through careful and intelligent investing in real estate!

Here's what happened. Back in May, 1985, a company named Oerlikon qualified for the short list for a $600 million air defence system for the Canadian forces. It doesn't sound too impressive, does it? But wait! *Wait*!!

In September of that same year, a parcel of land in St-Jean, Quebec, was valued at about $415,000. Yet by January of 1986, *it sold for nearly twice that sum!!*

Pas mal, eh? You see, earlier that same month, the president of that aerospace firm had expressed interest in the land! In fact, the company told me (at that time, the St-Jean Member of Parliament), that if it won the federal contract, it would build a plant there!

See what I mean? You have to keep your ears and eyes open, when it comes to successful real estate dealing. And it doesn't hurt to have friends higher up either, if you know what I mean. You do know what I mean, don't you?

Well, the next thing I did was to lobby the city council of St-Jean to rezone the property from residential to industrial! And how could I lose? Without that rezoning, Oerlikon might have built its plant somewhere else, and where there are plants, there are jobs, *oui? Oui!!*

Anyway, by late January, 1986, the land was now close to $3 million in value, since it was being flipped more times than a porpoise chorus line. By June of 1986, Oerlikon signed its defence contract with Ottawa, a business partner of mine gets close to one million smackers, and we are In Like Flynn!!

And there you have it! There's *big money* to be made in real estate, and *I can show you how to do it*!

— THERE'S POTENTIAL FOR HIGH PROFITS!
— YOU NEED TO KNOW THE RIGHT LOCATION! (Oerlikon sure did.)
— KNOW HOW TO PICK WINNERS!
— GET YOUR PROPERTY APPRAISED!
— DISCOVER HIGH PROFITS FROM UNDEVELOPED LAND!
— LEARN THE PAY-OFF IN COMMERCIAL PROPERTY!!
— AND WHAT ABOUT ZONING? THERE CAN BE HUGE PROFITS FROM CHANGING A PROPERTY'S USE!! (Look at how well I did with Oerlikon!)
— PROFIT GREATLY WHEN YOU SELL!
— THERE'S HIGH YIELDS IN INDUSTRIAL PROPERTY!!
— And most important of all: *Don't tell Brian*!!

Look, I'm just one man; *un petit gars* who was just in the right place at the right time. But *you can be too*! Learn from my experience!! I ended up making close to $400,000 from this deal — and *you can do the same*.

Mail a self-addressed stamped envelope to me and learn more! And remember:

ONLY ONE CANADIAN IN A THOUSAND WILL ANSWER THIS AD — YET THAT ONE WILL MOST CERTAINLY GET RICH!!

Write soon. It can get pretty lonely in solitary confinement.

Straight from the Faux Pas

SUZANNE BLAIS-GRENIER

I've had it with politics. I'm going to open a travel agency.

Straight from the Depths of Defeat

JAMES LEE

How was I to know that the federal government was hated so much by Prince Edward Islanders? I don't see what's so nasty about Brian doubling the entry fee to the P.E.I. national park, and raising the return fare on the ferries to the mainland. I mean, these are financially tough times.

And how was I to know that the farmers were all upset, just because it cost them five cents a pound to grow potatoes, and the best they could sell them for was one cent a pound? It certainly wasn't my fault. To paraphrase a one-time Prime Minister of Canada, it's not my job to sell their potatoes. Although, I have to admit, I never could figure out how they could make a living selling at those prices.

And how was I to know that Islanders would be upset when I accepted a free Florida vacation back in 1984? Everyone wants to get off the Island once in a while, especially when the weather turns rotten. True, the freebie was from Bernie Dale, who developed that fabulous hotel and convention centre on the Charlottetown waterfront, which I rescued with around $9 million, and which the province ended up selling for $1 million. But everyone makes mistakes.

And back in April, 1986, the people of Prince Edward Island made theirs. They elected some lousy Liberal to office, and bounced me and the provincial Tories out.

Enough is enough. They won't have James Lee to kick around anymore. Especially those women with their high heels; they really hurt. The gals had it in for me, and all I said was that they should shut up, take low pay and vote Tory.

Anyway, this island is too small for a guy like me. An island of 125,000 people, with fewer voters than the number of shoppers in the West Edmonton Mall on a slow day, doesn't deserve the kind of leadership I've given them.

I'm moving on. Prince Edward Island is small potatoes.

DON GETTY

Dedicated to the Eskimo old-timers

It's early in the first quarter of my leadership of the province of Alberta, so there's not much for me to say. What's really worth writing about was that incredible game of November 24, 1956 — a date burned into the memories of every Canadian as deeply as the hanging of Louis Riel and the dismantling of the N.E.P. — when a Canadian quarterback won the Grey Cup. And the Canadian quarterback was me, Donald Getty. The Eskimos made 36 first downs, nearly all of them rushing. We ran 121 plays, rushing 83 times for 456 yards. Every one still remains a record in the annals of the Canadian Football League. We beat the Montreal Alouettes by a score of 50 to 27. Sure, I broke my nose, but that's what sports are all about. And politics too, as I am quickly discovering. But we've got to balance that damned budget, and that's that.

I was first sent into the Game of Life in 1933 in Westmount, Quebec, although I never lived there long enough to become an Alouette fan, Allah be praised. We soon rushed to London, Ontario, where I was a quarterback in high school, occasionally catching a class or two. As a teenager, I usually scored with the girls. I mean, with all that I knew about making passes, how could I lose?

I then attended the University of Western Ontario, tackling some stupid course or other, while leading the Mustangs to two championships. When I graduated *Summa Cum Laude*, a relatively obscure academic honour compared to most yards gained passing, my football coach worked out a job with Imperial Oil, a company with a good punting average in the oil fields.

But who the hell wants to live in Sarnia? The only football team around is the Imperials, and who do *they* play? Anyway, I'd been drafted by the Edmonton Eskimos, and I never would have forgiven myself if I hadn't tried for the first down there.

So I headed west, as hundreds of thousands of other Easterners did in those years, with my new bride. I ended up playing a full decade with the Eskimos, quarterbacking in three Grey Cup games.

In 1959, I was named the outstanding player in the West, which pointed to a future career in politics. (Peter Lougheed, who also went into politics, was merely a scatback with the Eskies; he wasn't anything special on the field, but did O.K. in politics, as some may realize. He's now sitting pretty on the bench, if you could call being a director for two dozen different companies being on the bench. Not a bad act to follow.)

It's been all downhill since then, to tell the truth. It was sad, but I had to hold down a job during the week, to make ends meet. One could say that they were tight ends, in fact. I was still working for Imperial, and when I finally gave up the ball in 1964, I began my own oil and gas company. (You didn't need ten other guys on your team, back then, to make it in the energy business.)

I met Peter Lougheed in late 1965, and we hit it off really well, in spite of his inferior record on the field. He urged me to run for a seat in the provincial legislature, and I was one of the first half-dozen members on the team opposing the Socreds in the Centennial Year.

After we rushed to victory four years later, I was named Minister of Intergovernmental Affairs, and in 1975, I became the Minister of Energy. And with the energy that I showed on the field for the Eskimos, who could blame Peter for choosing me again and again to play for him?

Lougheed and I played political ball together for years. The only problem is, the Feds didn't know how to play ball fairly. They kept fouling and fumbling the pigskin. I usually managed to intercept them, before they could do any more damage to the Edmonton team, but Ottawa kept changing the rules after the game had begun. I reached the point of calling Time Out.

I finally left politics in 1979, having been an active player on Lougheed's team for a dozen years. Like most former politicians, I took advantage of my years in government, and soon became the Chairman and C.E.O. of Nortek Energy Corp, and began to pick up more directorships than first downs. But when Peter hung up his shoes in 1985, I wasn't about to sit on the bench anymore. I was still in shape, still capable of picking up some yardage on those rough riders out in Ottawa.

I had the fullbacking of most of my former teammates: Jackie Parker. Normie Kwong. Mike Volvan. Bib Kimoff. Even Dave

Fennell and Neil Lumsden, who played later and less well, but were still former members of the Greatest Team of All.

In November of 1985, Peter had the wind knocked out of him, and I took his place on the field. It's good to be quarterbacking again, after protecting Lougheed on every flank for those many years.

How can I describe how important those years of football have been to my physical and mental make-up? There was a closeness, a sense of teamwork which is hard to explain to those who haven't been out there, sweating, hitting, injuring, maiming. And the thrill of patting another football player on the rear is one which I'll never forget.

It's teamwork. That's what it's all about. You might get your faced shoved in the mud by Ottawa, but you simply get up and try again. I've tried to extend that teamwork beyond my close circle of advisors; for instance, I once attempted to complete a pass to my good friends and brown-eyed soul brother, Sheik Yamani, the Saudi Arabian Oil Minister. Once again, Ottawa tried to intercept. Jeez, I'm tired of them mucking up the game!

I've got the play book. I'm the quarterback. I'm ready to set some new records for service for most field goals in oil discovery; for most touchdowns in energy deals; for most points on the Oil and Gas Index; for most cutbacks in grants to hospitals, municipalities, school boards and universities. Hell, if those guys need more money, let them create a more winning budget. True, it may be the fourth quarter in those oil talks with the Feds in Ottawa, but I've got lots of time-outs left. And anyway, this ain't just provincial politics we're talking about here.

It's football.

Straight from Being Cut Off at the Pass

MICHEL GRATTON

Can't anyone take a joke anymore? Whatever happened to the good old days, when men were men and women were girls? If a guy can't ask a chick for a date anymore, then what has this world come to?

I mean, when they talk about "safe sex" nowadays, they don't *know* just how safe a guy has to be around Ottawa, at least.

I may have been Brian's press secretary, but it became pretty clear to me that I'd better not press too much, or the girls will start screaming "pig."

Okay. The broads won. From now on, when a bimbo reporter asks for an interview with Mulroney, she might get flowers and candy from me, but no more than that. My lips are sealed.

If they want dates, they'll have to check the Companions Wanted in the *Globe and Mail*.

SONDRA GOTLIEB

Dear Beverly,

Imagine how charmed I was, when asked by this major Canadian publisher — as if *any* Canadian publisher could be truly "major" — to write a brief autobiography about myself! I was fascinated to hear that there's this fad going on right now, up in Canada, for every politician in sight to write their life story! Isn't that a scream?! Anyway it sounds like fun, so here goes!!

They call us "Burns and Allen." They call us "Abbott and Costello." They call us "Mutt and Jeff." Since last March, they've been calling us "Leopold and Loeb," but I'd rather not talk about that right now.

It has been kind of strange, Beverly, to go from the Great White Nothing all the way to the peak of the earth's political firmament, so to speak, and become known as the stars of Washington. We are toasted by everyone who is anyone in the U.S. capital, and invitations to our parties have been known to be sold by scalpers for up to $1000 apiece! And that's *American* money. They love us down here, and that sure beats being ignored to death, back up in the North.

I guess I should go back to the beginning, Beverly. I was the only daughter of a middle-class Jewish family from Winnipeg's North End. My parents were really quite bright, even though I personally never could get the hang of studying. Or remembering names or faces either. It took ages to get over that rather embarrassing moment when I confused Henry Kissinger with the pudgy old German fellow who delivers our bagels on Sunday mornings. Why, he refused to deliver to the Embassy for three months, until I wrote out a formal apology on our ritzy stationery!

My father was born in Russia before the Revolution — thank God it wasn't after, Beverly — and went to Winnipeg, where he studied until he earned an MA in chemistry. My mother was born in Winnipeg, and was a teacher. And I? I'm not really brainy, I'm more the physical type, but I married an intelligent man didn't I? And that wasn't stupid!

He was the only son of a very rich Winnipeg family, and he zipped through Harvard Law School, won a Rhodes scholarship to Oxford to study international law, taught, became a barrister in London's Inner Temple, and then showed real brain power by marrying me.

His name — and since 1955, mine, giggle giggle — was Allan Gotlieb, which means "love of God," as in the common Washington expression, "For the love of God, what the hell is Sondra up to this week?" We met at a party — he was 26, I, a blushing, virginal 18 — dated a few weeks, and then he returned to England. His mummy and daddy invited me over for tea — and I didn't even know how to make tea, back then! — arranged a transatlantic call from their sweet only child while I was there, and we were suddenly engaged! This is known, in diplomatic circles, as a shidduch.

Within weeks, I was in Oxford, and in his arms, and not necessarily in that order. I learned to cook, how to talk, and how to keep up with this brilliant, brilliant man.

By 1960, Allan's marvelous career at External Affairs had begun. He was quite a feather in their cap; Canada had never had anyone really intelligent work for them before. Our first posting was in Geneva, which is overseas, if I remember correctly. We had three children — all three have his brains, thank God — and lots and lots of fun. I learned how to leave the table promptly with the other girls, when the wine was passed around. I learned that the ladies' toilets have stalls, and the men's toilets, those strange, vertical things that I once thought were washbasins. In short, I learned how to be the wife of a rapidly-rising diplomat.

But I learned so much more, over in Geneva, Beverly! While Allan served as the first secretary at the Canadian mission to the United Nations over there, I became fluent in French — always an asset in Canada, really! — and learned a lot about art, culture and cuisine, also not necessarily in that order.

By 1965, we were back in Ottawa, where Allan headed External Affairs' legal division. Within two years, he was promoted to the assistant undersecretary level, and Pierre Trudeau met him and was as impressed as I still am. Thank God that fellow is no longer in power, Beverly! It's true, he has really helped spark our joint career, but Ronnie Reagan just hated him!

Anyway, by 1968, Allan and I were deputy minister of Communications, and then deputy minister of Manpower and Immigration, and then, in 1977, Undersecretary of State for External Affairs. Allan published a number of really important books on international affairs, although, to tell the truth, Bev, my books have always sold a lot better. Of course, mine are more accessible. You don't need a genius-level I.Q. to understand them. I mean, I'm no genius either.

And what did little wifey do, during these years that Allan was scaling the slimy walls of Ottawa politics? (Hey, I like that metaphor! I think I'll use it in my next book.) I became known as a first-rate party-giver and a disarming hostess, although I've since learned that the only really first-rate parties are in Washington.

True, I failed my courses at Carleton, as noted above, but I did lots of other great things: I was a volunteer canvasser for the Ottawa Community Chest, until I threw out the receipts by mistake; learned to play tennis, and, thanks to Allan's prodding, began to write books. Oh, Beverly! I'd found my niche at last!

Since all I knew about was food, I hooked up with Oberon Press — the owners were my neighbours in Rockcliffe — and had published *The Gourmet's Canada* and *Cross Canada Cooking*. Not haute cuisine; maybe, but pretty haute stuff, if I say so myself. Then I wrote *True Confections*, a semi-autiobiographical book which actually won the Stephen Leacock Medal for Humour in Canada! Leacock was the only Canadian author that you Americans ever knew about, until Peggy Atwood and Robbie Davies — I've had both for dinner, I'll have you know — although the award is really no honour; they usually give it only to books which are distinctly not funny. We Canadians are that way.

Then, Allan and I got posted to Washington! Oh, Beverly, it was wonderful!

And the parties! One this night for 150; one the next night for 275; one Saturday night for 180. I wouldn't mind so much if Allan and I were merely attending them. But we had to throw them!

I've learned so much, Beverly! I've learned so very, very much! For instance, never but never sit Cap Weinberger next to Alexander Haig! It's kind of like sitting a convicted rapist next to his victim, and I am not going to tell you which one was which.

It's just non-stop. David Brinkley is a regular, although in many ways, I prefer him on TV where I can turn him off. Ed Meese isn't as awful as he looks, nor is Scotty Reston as cute as he looks. And

Michael Deaver just wants money, money, money, and that's all there is to it. Sometimes I feel as though he's running a protection racket, and not merely a lobbying outfit.

All this throwing of parties — oh my God, I almost typed throwing of punches! Isn't the mind an extraordinary thing? — has really cut down my time to write. But I managed to write *First Lady, Last Lady*, back in 1981, and *Wife Of*, just last year. And I do have my regular column in *The Washington Post*, poking fun at embassy life.

It's really super here, Beverly, despite that incident with my secretary! And best of all: Allan and I are being paid in real, American dollars! It's the only way to live, really, in Washington, or anywhere else. I recommend it to everyone, back home. And how can they *not* love Allan and me, up in Canada? We've made our country famous once more, and without a single snowstorm, or goal scored! Take that, Wayne Grentny, or whoever you are!

Love,
Sondra

P.S. Guess what Beverly — we might be moving soon. I understand the Beirut Phalangists throw some *wild* parties!

Straight from the Symbol

JEAN DORÉ

It happened in Spain: Juan Carlos replaced Franco, and brought democracy to that tortured land.

It happened in the Phillipines: Corazon Aquino replaced Ferdinand Marcos, and brought democracy to that tortured land.

It happened in the United States: Ronald Reagan replaced Jimmy Carter, and brought trading arms for terrorists to a country that used to shake its fists at terrorists, bringing democracy to the tortured lands of Iran and Nicaragua.

And it happened in Montreal!! I, Jean Doré, brought symbolism back to that tortured city. I unlocked the huge oak front doors of the city hall in Old Montreal! I agreed to have *committee meetings*, where ordinary citizens could actually visit, and have their say! I froze transit fares! I abolished Montreal's water tax! I, uh, I, uh . . .

True, there have been a few *minor* irritations, such as the refusal of myself and the half-dozen members of the executive committee of the Montreal Citizens' Movement to ever meet with the press; the $1.44-billion budget (which *was* less than 8% over Drapeau's last one, I'll have you know); Pierre Le Francois's $120,000 salary as the Secretary General in charge of administration, which made him the best-paid municipal civil servant in Canada; the $24,500 we gave Assistant Secretary General Pierre Beaudet to move from Quebec City to Montreal, on top of his $80,000 a year salary, etc. etc.

But we had always *promised* to spread the money around when the MCM took over. We just didn't say who would get it.

GRANT DEVINE

Louis XIV believed in Divine Right, and, in their own particular fashion, so do the people of Saskatchewan.

I was born in 1944 in Lake Valley, on a farm that had been in the family for three generations. Seeing the great future that farming held for its adherents, I headed off to university as fast as I could, getting a B.A. at U. of S., then two Master's degrees in agricultural economics and business administration at the University of Alberta, and finally a Ph.D. in the same subject at Ohio State University in Columbus, a southeastern suburb of Moose Jaw. (For those of you unfamiliar with the term, "agricultural economics" is what is commonly referred to as an oxymoron, in the honoured tradition of "airplane food," "married bachelor" and "honest Socialist.")

Once again feeling the ancient pull of the land in my soul, I joined the University of Saskatchewan as an associate professor of agricultural economics, an esoteric field which I've just explained.

My earliest years in politics were tinged with great anticipation. By that I mean that I kept losing, and wondered what it would be like to win.

I have always believed in sound politics, and when I first ran as a Conservative in the provincial riding of Saskatoon Nutana in 1978, I was defeated soundly by my NDP opponent.

Then, two years later I ran again, in a by-election in Estevan, when once again I was creamed by my Socialist rival. This in itself wouldn't have been too bad, except that I had won the leadership of the Saskatchewan Tories a year earlier, which meant that I was unable to lead my party in the provincial House. This unhappy fact moved many to give me the nickname "The Invisible Man," even though my resemblance to Claude Rains is really rather slight.

So, imagine the surprise of everyone when I led my party to the biggest landslide victory in the history of my beloved province in 1982, with 55 of the 64 seats. I was finally able to take a seat as the Premier, which was a great relief; I'd grown tired of standing around outside the legislative building in Regina.

This victory was all the more impressive, since Saskatchewan has a tragic history of socialism, which must be rooted out, like a diseased tree. (I told you that I come from a long line of farmers.) It's true, the NDP made some rather foolish mistakes in that campaign, but the real reason for my glorious victory was in my own inspired promises. I offered to abolish gasoline taxes (most farms use gas in their tractors) and reduce mortgage rates (most farms are mortgaged up to their cows, as well as their asses). The Socialists, in their traditionally exciting fashion, had offered to lower freight rates, which enthralled the dozens of people in Saskatchewan who actually cared.

The people loved me for other important reasons as well, such as my constant reminding of our citizens that I had a rural past: I used to wear tattered shirts, torn pants, no shoes, and carried a well-dressed Toronto banker around on my shoulders.

I also used to sprinkle phrases like "you betcha!" and "ain't it the truth!" in my speeches, which impressed most farmers, but it moved my examiners at Ohio State to ask me to return my Ph.D. to them. Furthermore, I continue to hold the Agriculture portfolio, along with my Premiership, which sure beats having to get a job on the farm.

It has to be admitted, my massive majority over the NDP slipped somewhat in the provincial election of October, 1986: But I still won a commanding popular vote of 45%, over the miniscule 45% of the Socialists. Thank heavens, not to mention gerrymandering, that my 45% gave my Tories 38 seats to the NDP's 25. The Liberals, some fringe party which I had never heard of before, managed to win one.

But the fact remains, I managed to win the second straight Conservative election in the history of this socialist-stained province! Did you know that as recently as 1971, my party was winning only one vote out of ever 50 cast?? I didn't know it either, but I have some great researchers on staff.

No, I've proven to the thousands of people living right across this financially — and geographically — flat province that April 26, 1982, was no fluke. I've done *everything* big: I managed to turn an old-fashioned balanced budget from Blakeney into over $2 billion in debts. And, more important, I managed to get Brian to promise a billion smackers in farm loans, just before the election, which didn't hurt a bit when the farmers got to the polling booths.

Then there was my $282 million housing program offering cheap mortgages for up to ten years; tenure loans of up to $10,000 at 6%, and $1500 grants for home repairs. And how about my pension program for homemakers and part-time workers? More progressive than conservative, eh??

It's the old story: With enough socialist ideas, and enough deficit spending, Tories can hang onto power forever. And for two straight elections, I've been kicking Saskatchewan NDPers in the potash, right across the province.

ROCHE LASALLE

Let's get one thing straight: If we don't *all* go out and hire ex-cons, then who's going to do it? Don't these poor, misunderstood men and women deserve a second chance? I mean, Christ, didn't the entire country keep giving Trudeau and *his* henchmen second and third chances back in 1972, 1974 and 1980?

But now, I guess it's time for the truth to come out as to why I was a "minister without portfolio": It was stolen.

Straight from the Greatest City on Earth

JEAN DRAPEAU

DEDICATION

This autobiography of His Honour, Mayor Jean Drapeau of Montreal, Province of Quebec, the World's Greatest Metropolis, is dedicated to Papa Doc Duvalier and Cecil B. DeMille, two men who also reached for greatness.

The French-Canadian people are royalists, I have often said. What they want is a king. Well, this is what they have got, almost non-stop, since 1954 (with a brief interregnum which I have no need to discuss), thanks to their good faith in me. The fact that I had to go frequently through the indignity of an election — something no king should ever have to worry about — certainly counts in my favour.

The citizens who kept re-electing me with overwhelming majorities have not been interested in discussions, but in results. And results is what they have received: Superhighways. The Montreal subway system. Place Des Arts. Expo 67. The 1976 Summer Olympics. The World Trade Centre. The CN Tower. Buckingham Palace. The Pyramids of Egypt. L'Hermitage. The Great Wall of China. Well, most of them, anyway.

I was born in the natural way in Rosemount, a suburb of The Most Magnificent City on Earth — although it wasn't that way then — on February 18, 1916, today, a municipal holiday in Montreal. My mother was Berthe Martineau; my father, Joseph Napoleon Drapeau. You can guess which one inspired me the most. I have always been proud that my ancestors were among the first settlers who came with Maisonneuve to found Ville Marie, where the extraordinary City of Montreal now stands. The fact that they were not the first settlers to found Ville Marie has been a source of continual pain to me, not unlike the existence of Maurice Duplessis, but there wasn't much to be done about him, either.

Jean-de-Brébeuf and Le Plateau schools had the honour of having me in their classes, as did the professors at the University of

Montreal, in 1935. By 1937, I had a diploma in Social Economics and Political Science, and in the following year, a degree in Arts. These were hard times so I had to take a part-time job in the City Welfare Department to support myself, while studying in law school. In January, 1943, when Our Boys were valiantly fighting a struggle to the death against the Evils of Conscription, I was admitted to the Montreal bar.

By 1948, I was famous for my series of articles in *Le Devoir*, exposing the dreadful plight of workers suffering from silicosis, which was one hellova lot better than exposing myself to silicosis. And the following year, I fought for the workers who had been arrested during the Asbestos strike. It was then that I realized something truly important: no future monument that I would build would ever have any asbestos in it. That stuff can kill you.

I was a demon! I wrote a devastating series of articles exposing the monstrous amount of criminial activity in my beloved City, and the problems with the police department. Why, my work was so extraordinary, there was a judicial probe, starring me and a handful of lesser prosecutors.

Then, something happened which has proven to be the greatest moment in Montreal history. I put together a loose reform coalition called the Civic Action league, with myself as candidate for mayor. The people finally saw the Light, and I was elected! I was 38, and was the youngest mayor in the history of the City.

It was a living hell at first. The City Hall had 99 members in its council, which was too much of a bad thing. It was a bureaucratic nightmare, and my brilliant leadership was stifled. I soon discovered that my power was terribly limited, which, of course, is no way to successfully run the most magnificent City on the face of the Earth.

Then, alas, I came into conflict with Le Chef. Duplessis and I had a slight disagreement over a slum-clearance project, and he threw the entire resources of his *Union Nationale* organization behind his own candidate for mayor, the bugger. I lost by 4,000 votes, but it was the City of Montreal that lost, as we all know today.

Did I quit? No. I made speeches across the province, and even published a book filled with my glorious insights, *Jean Drapeau Vous Parle*, which was an instant best-seller, probably because of the title.

I also broke with the Civic Action league, which had been cramping my style. I began to track down dozens of lawyers and businessmen, many of whom had never been active in politics before, and they all readily agreed to join my new Montreal Civic party. And it worked!! My new party formed Montreal's first majority government, with 46 out of 66 members in the newly-reconstructed Council.

At last, I could take the action my people had longed for! I flew to England and France, interviewing experts on police reform and made a sweeping overhaul of our cops.

Then I began to study subway systems all over the world. I made personal trips, at great hardship to myself and at great expense to our City's budget, to study the Paris Metro and the London tube, and I learned remarkable things: the food is *much* better in France than in England, but the British are a lot friendlier.

I came back to my beloved City, convinced that the Montreal Metro should run on rubber wheels, and in troughs of reinforced concrete, rather than the New York system (where, I might add, both the food and the people are nasty). Did the critics howl! It won't work, they cried. It'll be too expensive, they shouted! The expensive part isn't important, so I won't comment on that. But did it work? Why, the Montreal Metro has been described as the most comfortable and the quietest subway system on Earth! And with its employees on strike for much of each year, it is getting quieter every day.

By 1962, I was hitting my stride, in terms of elections. I won a four-year term with 90% of the vote. My Civic party took 41 out of 45 seats, which made me happy, but still troubled. Who were these other four people, and who on earth was voting for them? This would have to stop.

By 1973, I had completed the Place Des Arts, one of my many monuments to the arts. And the reconstruction of Dorchester Boulevard, a project going back to my first term, was also near completion. No wonder they kept re-electing me by such huge margins!

What are dreams? Dreams are merely those things which we haven't managed to turn into reality yet. By the early 1960s, I was determined to have my wonderful City be chosen as the site for the International World's Fair in 1967. The federal government, as always, was asleep at the wheel. So I flew off to make my own, personal representation on behalf of my magnificent City, before the Bureau of International Expositions in Paris. Once again, the food was superb, the people difficult. But at least they were not stupid; soon after my landslide of 1962, Montreal was chosen as the location for Expo 67.

I was inspired! I decided that it should be built on two artificial islands, and the critics mocked me! But who would know more about artificiality than Jean Drapeau? As I had promised, Expo opened on schedule, with 62 countries represented. It was my 100th birthday gift to Canada, and my own personal gift to the world, and the 50 million people who attended seemed to be pleased. Jean Drapeau, and Montreal, had triumphed again!

But Great Men never stop. I created a gigantic redevelopment of the downtown area of Montreal, including my brilliant double core — a network of underground shopping plazas. By sheer coincidence, another election took place shortly after the opening of Expo 67, and I won 95% of the vote this time, with my Civic Party winning 45 out of 48 wards. But why did my opponents still have 3 seats? Why? Why? Why?

Montreal was quickly becoming the most exciting Place on Earth to live, work, visit. Why, even mailing a letter in the late 1970s could be a thrilling experience. And when Charles de Gaulle visited the Fair and asked for a drink — it was "Cuba Libre" he said, not "Quebec Libre" — it was I who gave it to him.

My critics could play dirty, such as the time that they bombed my house and wrecked a classy restaurant I had just opened, but I wouldn't stand for any of their guff. In the 1970 election, I demolished a minor opposition movement, the *Front d'Action Politiique* (FRAP), winning 92% of the vote. And every one of the 52 Civic Party candidates were elected. At last!

That same year, I let the people know about my latest and greatest plan — until that date: the Montreal Summer Olympics for 1976. As always, I appeared in person before the International Olympic Committee. Just as I had won over the hearts, minds and votes of my citizens of Montreal; just as I had won over the Bureau of International Expositions in Paris, I wowed them at the Olympics. When one idiot doubted my proposal, I gave him my best and wittiest put-down: "Do you seriously doubt my City's ability to stage the Olympic games? You doubt my word? Me?" The committee gave me a standing ovation.

The Montreal Olympics went perfectly, of course. True, the federal government kept delaying necessary legislation, which made the construction rather tight, and there were a number of minor labour stoppages, but in retrospect it was really nothing. There were few deficits, and these will probably be picked up by our grandchildren and great-grandchildren, in loving remembrance for a magnificent summer of games. My critics like to mock my *bon mot* about "The Montreal Summer Olympics will no sooner have a deficit than a man will have a baby," but they all forgot one thing: Morgentaler has been operating freely in Quebec for many, many years.

Oh, I could list the many other extraordinary accomplishments of my reign, from the Picasso exhibit to the Jazz Festivals, to the Fireworks Exhibition to the display of Ancient Egyptian artifacts. But it would run on for hundreds of pages, and that would be excessive.

Anyway, at the time I write, I have won seven straight elections. I have survived six prime ministers, and Quebec has had eight premiers. Toronto, a minor suburb to the west, has had nine mayors. The Civic Party has been like a delightful private club, never having to trouble itself with boring policy discussions, never wasting time with the nominating of candidates. It has been a joy to be able to reward my friends for their favours; I trust that they would do the same for me, were they in absolute power.

I cannot take all the credit for the Greatness of Montreal; indeed, were it not for the credit advanced by the banks, many of my astonishing projects would never have seen fruition. But I think that we can truly compare the grandeur of Montreal to that of ancient Athens. Two thousand, five hundred years ago, Pericles, too, was criticized for building the Acropolis. And, to the best of my knowledge, he never managed to finish *its* retractable roof, either.

Finally, in late May, 1986, I decided that I would not run again. I probably could have wheeled, and still won the mayoralty one last time, but I'd had enough.

But I can assure you: it was only failing health that could ever, ever, ever force me from the political arena.

That and people calling me *Monsieur le Merde*.

Straight from the Side of the Defence

PERRIN BEATTY

Have you detected a pattern here? I keep taking over from much older cabinet ministers who have screwed things up, and am expected to clean up their mess after them. It's not easy, being one of the youngest kids around the House.

When Elmer MacKay, Mulroney's first solicitor-general, was discovered having stupid tête-à-têtes with Disco Dick Hatfield, who was under investigation by the RCMP at the time, I got *his* portfolio. I wasn't even a lawyer, but I did a better job than any ambulance-chaser could have done.

Then, since the summer of '86, I've been in charge of the defence portfolio, once again replacing a man who was slightly out of favour (not to mention out of whack) — Erik Nielsen. But he was a former bomber pilot, and the last time I'd worn a uniform was when I was a cadet at Upper Canada College!!

No sweat. I'm as daring as my tastebuds. (I lunch on turkey sandwiches on white bread, followed by a few shots of milk.) And more important, I get around. I've visited our troops right across Canada and even Europe, although I never did track down that great bar in Germany that Bob Coates told me about.

And now, I'm working hard on a White Paper on defense. Actually, considering the size of our disarmed forces, maybe that should read "white flag." But it'll be done, by gum. We've got the new uniforms, and all we need are a few new battleships that can't be confused with submarines, which has been the problem in the past, and we can really get cracking.

I plan to support our boys in green, or whatever colour it is now. And I want to get all the citizens of this great land behind them, as well. After all, it's not easy for a few hundred men and women to defend a country as big as this one.

Yes, we'll soon have that White Paper on defence. Or we will, if only Brian would stop moving me around. The problem is, every other Minister is a lot older than me, and they keep screwing up, so he needs me.

And when Brian calls, I'm there: True, proud and free. As for the North, I'll have to see if we've got any men and weapons to spare. Or disarming ladies, for that matter.

Straight from the Speaker's (Silenced) Mouth

JOHN BOSLEY

Of *course* I'm not bitter that I'm no longer the Speaker of the House of Commoners, or whatever the hell it's called.

Why should I mind being forced to move out of Kingsmere, and having my salary tumble from $115,000 down to $73,000?

And what's so special about being pushed out of a job by Brian Mulroney?

Hell, millions of Canadians in all walks of life can say the same thing.

FLORA MACDONALD

Sorry I got to this in to the publisher so late; I just got off the phone to an old pal in Sydney. How on earth was I to know that she'd be asleep? It's only 2:30 A.M. Oh, dear. There's a time difference, isn't there? Well, anyway, even 3:30 A.M. isn't that late. In fact, some people would call that rather early, depending on which way you're coming from. And I, personally, am coming from the left-wing of the federal Progressive Conservative Party, where I have been a major force for truth, justice and the Canadian way, since my first election to Parliament, back in 1972.

It's really been a Cinderella story, my life, except there's been no castle, no prince, and I never had any evil step-sisters — unless you count some of the Grits I've been forced to work with. But everything else has been pretty parallel to that classic Canadian folk tale: Back in the 1950s, I was making 140 smackers a month, typing; in 1979, I was making $60,000 a year, as the first female Secretary of State for External Affairs; in 1987, I'm making even more than that, as the Minister of Communications. And who communicates better than me, especially on the telephone? Actually, when you consider the Liberal-caused inflation since I was a secretary, I'm still making about the same salary. But the honour is so much more, to be a VIP in Ottawa! Well, okay, maybe if you're a man, it is. But it's getting better all the time! I *swear* it is!

Well, I *think* it is.

I was born 61 years ago in North Sydney, Nova Scotia, out on Cape Breton. I was the third of six children. We were all taught tolerance, decency, humanitarianism and kindness — things the federal Liberals could learn a thing or two about. My grandfather was the captain of a clipper ship, and my grandmother actually used to sail with him. (She didn't trust him to go out without her around. You know what men are like.) But I found that terribly romantic, and it filled me with a longing to travel. Who knew that it would take me to the capitals of the world? Glace Bay. Kingston, Ontario. Ottawa. God, I still get the willies, just *thinking* about it.

My father, Fred MacDonald, was a Western Union telegraph

operator, which also made me fall in love with long distance. He was the greatest influence in my life, as he took us all to political rallies, used to recite poetry to us, helped us with our homework, and even shared the housework with my mother. No wonder I love Joe Clark so. The only difference was, you just couldn't get quiche in Cape Breton, growing up in the Great Depression. We didn't even know what quiche *was*.

Back in the early '40s in Sydney, women didn't go to college. In fact, we weren't even women, as I recall; we were girls. (That hasn't changed much, either.) When I graduated from North Sydney High School, I attended Empire Business College in 1943, which was one of the *worst* places to meet men on the face of the earth. I then landed my first job as a bank clerk. After that job, even Ottawa would be exciting. Well, a *little* more exciting.

By the age of 25, my father urged me to see the world, and that is exactly what I did: I herded sheep in Scotland, where I spoke the language so well; I ran a social club in London, where I didn't; I built sets for London theatres; I hitchhiked through Europe with friends; I picked grapes in Portugal; I even did maintenance in a convent in Rome. You might think this reads pretty funny on a resumé, but look at Pierre Trudeau: He never worked a day in his life before he became Prime Minister. And he didn't work a day in his life *after* he became Prime Minister, either. But I'm not bitter. The people just have to be educated, that's all. And as you can see from September, 1984, they *are* educable, after all.

When I returned to my Home and Native Land — just the thought of that line sends shivers up and down my spine, and it's a long spine, too — I was 28, and knew that I had to do something with my life. But I didn't want to do *too* much, so I went to Ottawa, where I applied for a secretarial job in External Affairs. (Who knew back then that I would some day be the boss of that amazing, important, and world-class department? Who knew that I would be the boss of that wonderful place for less than nine months?)

But I didn't get the position, since I was offered a typing job with the Progressive Conservative national headquarters while I was waiting. I stayed there for over a decade, working my way up to becoming the party's executive director. I was the centre of everything! "Ask Flora!" they would all cry. "Flora!" they would shout, "what is the party's stand on national defence?" "Only Flora would know the unemployment rate," they would admit. "Flora!" they would squeal, "I asked for double cream and no sugar, and you got it exactly right, once more. You're incredible!"

I was so incredible, in fact, that Dalton Camp let me in on a fascinating plan to rid the party of Mr. Crazyhead, John Diefenbaker. The latter was rather angry when he heard about my involvement with Dalton, but although he had me fired, he still showed affection for what I had done for the party. After all, did he not say that I was "the finest woman who ever walked the streets of Kingston"? (I'd moved to that lovely town in 1966.)

But I'd had enough of getting coffee for political leaders. I wanted to have someone else get *me* coffee for a change. So, after tutoring in the department of political science at Queen's University in Kingston for a while, I became involved in the Committee for an Independent Canada, and sought election in Kingston and the Islands. I wanted to fight for better recognition in Ottawa of what the rest of the country was like. For instance, the fact that Cape Breton is out in the Maritimes. And that the West could be taken for granted, since it was already strongly anti-Liberal. I also wanted to protect Canada's cultural identity. We had to make Canada safe for *King of Kensington* and re-runs of *Country Hoedown*. And where on earth was Juliette, now that we needed her more than ever?

I've been the Progressive Conservative Member of Parliament for my riding since 1972, and I've frankly done a marvelous job. I had no female political mentor — although there were some male MPs with leanings that I'd better not put in writing. Yet I was encouraged in my career by Ellen Fairclough, who had been appointed Canada's first woman cabinet minister by my old friend Dief. She once gave me a copy of *Ask No Questions*, the bio of Agnes McPhail, Canada's first MP of the female sex. The first stirring of deeply-felt feminism occurred in my breast. I knew, once and for all time, that *we girls had to stick together*.

I felt that politics had become too impersonal. So I struggled to make it otherwise. For instance, when I was asked about the Soviet domination of its European satellites, I told the questioner about my travels throughout Finland, and how lovely the people were. When I was asked about prison reform, I told the reporter about my years of volunteer work for the Elizabeth Fry Society. When I was asked about the huge expense accounts of the heads of cer-

51

tain missions in Europe, I told the challengers that I live frugally. I still feel the same way, after 15 years in Ottawa: *Nothing* is too difficult that cannot be made *personal*.

The greatest excitement of my life — with the exception of listening to the Mormon Tabernacle Choir on my car's tape cassette machine — was when I was named Canada's first female Secretary of State for External Affairs in the Cabinet of Joe Clark. True, the job didn't last very long, but that wasn't *my* fault!

There were great highlights during those exciting days (as opposed to exciting *years*): The time I was travelling in Africa with Prime Minister Clark and visited Cameroon, which I had *always* thought was a type of cookie. He went into a room to meet with that country's leader and foreign ministers. (Yes, it's a *country*!) Then I was told to go into another room, where the wives of the leaders could meet. "Would you mind waiting with the other women?" I was asked. It was a cute mistake, really, except that it was the *Canadian* ambassador who said it to me. To be fair, communication is *always* a problem in government. That's one more reason why I'm so pleased to be the Communications Minister.

And what of the time of the Iranian hostage-taking, when I spent three months secretly living with the daily tension of knowing that the lives of the 15 Canadians and their six American vistors were at risk in Teheran? And after the affair was over, I was asked by a reporter of the male sex, "How was a woman able to keep a secret like that?" Now *is that nice*?

Or the time at the United Nations, when I was introduced to the Pope as the *wife* of the Canadian Minister of External Affairs. That one truly hurt. If I were really married, what chances would I ever have of landing a job as a priest, after my political days are over? It's bad enough that I'm a woman.

The other special time, which I don't like to talk about too much, was when I ran for the federal Progressive Conservative leadership in 1976. You couldn't blame me for trying: I get along with people so well, and my Red Tory leanings were attractive to so *many* members of the party. Everyone *loved* me! "Flora Power" buttons were everywhere! I hit nearly every city across Canada, from the Atlantic to the Pacific, and even a few A & P stores along the way. Everywhere I went, the people turned out in droves. I was not only supported by Tories, but even by NDPers and Liberals, who were clearly just *dying* to see a woman lead the Progressive Conservative Party. Why, even former Liberal cabinet minister Judy LaMarsh sent $500! (Sisterhood is Powerful, as we like to say in the Movement.)

Well, I didn't win, as everyone in Cameroon knows by now. Or should know. I was beaten by my (later) good friend Joe Clark, who ran this country so brilliantly, back in 1979 and 1980. It was such a *thrill* to hear from women delegates, who used to come up to me and say, "I'd *love* to vote for you, but I'll have to ask my husband." The only problem was, what if the husband said "no"?

I think he did. And so *many* people had promised to vote for me, who didn't! That *wasn't* very good of them, don't you agree? I felt betrayed. Let down. Double-crossed. Crushed. Squished. Devastated. Wiped out. Yes, I even went out and bought a new thesaurus, just to try to capture my feelings for this autobiography.

In the Great Cabinet Shuffle of 1986, I was moved from Manpower and Immigration over to Communications. It's for the best; there were so many leaks over at my Employment office, I began to think we were working in a washroom.

But I should have lots of fun with Communications, especially following Marcel, who did to the English language what Dief used to do to French.

And if anyone can talk, it's me.*

* Just as long as they don't force me to watch *too* many CBC-TV shows; as a woman and a Tory, I've been through enough pain in my life.

RICHARD HATFIELD

Sure, I've acted a bit dopey at times.   And maybe the smoke has gotten a bit thick around my political career. But there's no question about it: I'm the longest-serving premier in Canada, at this moment, having been riding high in the hearts, minds, and most importantly, votes, of New Brunswickers since November, 1970. And now that Bill Davis has stepped down — he was always four months behind me — I continue to bust all records.

My daddy was also into politics; in fact, he was a Progressive Conservative Member of Parliament in Ottawa, going off to that tedious town when I was only nine.   He discouraged all of us — I was the youngest of five — from entering politics, and he certainly succeeded; many of my critics insist that I haven't been in the New Brunswick legislature more than a few times a year since the early 1970s.

After high school, I went off to Acadia University in Wolfville, Nova Scotia, where I did a lot of performing in plays, knowing that this would stand me in good stead. It sure as heck didn't hurt Ronnie Reagan, did it?   I was first attracted to Liberal politics, may the good Lord forgive me, but then I discovered Robert Stanfield, and really got turned on by him; probably the first person since his wife who is willing to admit that.

In my law class at Dalhousie, the best student was John Crosbie, but I beat him out in criminal law. And thank heavens I did, since I've had a number of strange brushes with the law ever since, and it never hurts to know these things from the inside.

I tried Ottawa politics for a brief while, serving as executive assistant to the Federal Minister of Trade and Commerce in the late '50s, but I missed my beloved home province. So it was in good ol' N.B. that I planted my political roots; I've always preferred home grown.

I was elected MLA for Carleton County in 1961, became the leader of the Progressive Conservative opposition eight years later, and in 1970, at the tender age of 39, I became Premier of my native New Brunswick, when the Tories won the provincial election. What a score!!

It's been a wonderful 16 + years. I've hit so many highs   for the province of New Brunswick, that it's hard to be able to list them all. My mind keeps wandering, anyway. But I'll try:

• I brought a thrilling new sports car to the province, called The Bricklin, named after the brilliant entrepreneur and inventor of that bat-winged beauty. It never did work out, which is a real shame; it would have provided lots of jobs for my fellow New Brunswickers. But what a gorgeous car that was!!

• I helped create a magnificent nuclear power plant at Point Lepreau, which we began back in 1974. It was to cost around $400 million, and ended up costing about $1.4 billion. Which just goes to show that it's not only Jean Drapeau who can think big, is it?

• I made New Brunswick the only province that is officially bi-lingual, which was only the proper and ethical thing to do. By chance, it also liberated the French-speaking Acadian population from the evil of voting Grit, which they had been mistakenly doing for many years before.

• I made a big hit when I toasted Prince Charles and Princess Diana, when they visited our beautiful province during the summer of 1983. I'm not certain what I said back then;   come to think of it, I wasn't quite sure what I was saying at the time I said it, either. You see, I was just so excited that I was just floating!! Anyway, the British press nicknamed me "Disco Dick," which I thought was rather sweet; I vastly preferred that name to "Disco Duck," which I had been getting from the Fredericton and Moncton press, up to that point.

There have been some sad moments in my lengthy rein as well, such as that weird incident with the pot that had been planted in my luggage when the Queen was visiting, uh, er, uh, Fredericton during her royal tour in September, 1984. What a dirty trick. I'm the Premier of New Brunswick, not some dumb teenager growing his own behind his barn. You don't get to be leader over 700,000 Maritimers without a good dollop of taste.

THE CANADIAN DOLLAR

I'm glad to get my story into print before I am killed off at the end of this decade by that new, ugly, 11-sided coin that's not much bigger than a quarter. Of course, thanks to the incompetence of many of the men and women who share this volume with me, I'm not worth much more than a quarter, anyway.

It's been a full and rich life, pun intended. My ancestors came to this country in the form of beaver skins, also known as wampum. And even my great-great-great grandfather had an interesting history: until the fall of Quebec, in 1759, the French used to have "playing card money," which was produced by cutting up kings, queens and jacks into quarters, and using it for currency. Anyone who has ever lost his shirt at poker can relate to that.

My glory days, of course, were back when I could be converted into gold, before the First World War, and briefly in the late 20s and early 30s. Those were the times! I was honoured, praised, treated with respect! To tell the truth, it was my most individualistic period, since every bank was printing their own bank notes. Doctor Ruth doesn't know what Good Sex is, unless she's been in a wallet for a few days, rubbing up against a Bank of British Columbia dollar. God, they were good to the touch. The Bank of Winnipeg currency was pretty, but a bit flat. And talk about frigid.

Then that stinking Bank of Canada was set up by that loser R.B. Bennett — another Tory, God help me. And since then, it's been downhill all the way.

Actually, I didn't mind the Queen's face on my front; she was a looker, back in the 50s. But then, damn it, so was I. And I wasn't too hot about them putting all the colours into me, making me look like a bundle of Monopoly dollars on speed.

But what really burns my ass is what the feds have done to my value. Christ, I remember when I was worth a dollar and six cents, against my hot-shot cousin the Yankee dollar. But with Trudeau and his lackies printing me like I was going out of style, I began to phone my distant relatives in Argentina and Israel, to ask what it was like to be worthless. (Mark, a German ancestor on my mother's side, was so mortified back in the early 1920s, it took him a quarter-century and fifty million dead to recover. Never underestimate the value of a buck).

So now, what's happening? The Canadian dollar has become the peso of the North, with Japanese traders dumping me as if I were just trash. And maybe I am. If you were handled by as many men — and women — as I have been, you would feel dirty all over, too.

That's all I've got to say. I know my end is coming soon. But it's *not my fault.* It's those goddam Grits. And also, it's those bloody Tories. And the NDPers have done their part as well, especially when they had Trudeau in their pocket, back in the early 70s. I'm through with this country, and it's about time. A peso might be worth buggerall as well, but at least it's warm down there.

You Canucks know what you can do with your new "dollar coin." And since it'll be round and hard, it should be easier to stuff it there, too.

Straight from the B'y Who Builds the Boat

JOHN CROSBIE

Translated from the Newfoundland, by Joe Clark

I'm 56 now, and it sure looks like I'm never gonna become Prime
Minister of this great land. Lordy knows I've tried, that's for sure.
I was right up there at the top, and coulda beat Brian, but I just
could not get enough of the others to throw their lot with me.

Could it be because I couldn't speak French? No, that couldn't
be it; hardly anyone else in the PC caucus can speak it worth a
tinker's dam, either. Maybe it was because I couldn't speak English?
Who knows. Either way, I'm stuck here in the Justice portfolio,
surrounded by pimps, whores and homosexual soldiers.

It was a rough life, coming from a wealthy family in Newfoundland. Rough, because there's nothing much to buy out there,
and it can drive a man crazy. But I'm basically just a down-home,
outport, man of the people, in spite of my background. I'm like
most Newfoundland natives: I was educated at Bishop Field College, St. Andrew's, Queen's University where I won the University Medal in political science, Dalhousie where I won the University Medal in Law, and the University of London, where I never won
anything at all. Maybe that is why I refuse to speak English clearly.

I began my political career as a city councillor in St. John's, and
ended up holding half a dozen different cabinet posts in the Newfoundland legislature. I'm ashamed to admit it, but I was a Liberal
back then. It's not as painful as Kurt Waldheim 'fessing up to his
background, but it's still pretty awful.

I had a slight disagreement with the then-Premier Joey Smallwood,
and I crossed over to the Conservative side of the aisle. I had always
assumed that the Q.C. after my name meant Quick Change.

I've been a Member of Parliament in Ottawa since 1976, and
eagerly and proudly took up the Finance Minister's job for my good
friend Joe Clark, against whom I eagerly and proudly ran for the
leadership of the Progressive Conservatives, in 1983.

I was a masterful Minister of Finance, and I had lots of bright,
intelligent ideas which could have saved this country, after a dozen

years of disastrous leadership by the commie Grits. But no, I had to go ahead and raise the price of gas in gallons, instead of litres. What a stupid move! It really is the best argument for using metric I've ever heard; do you realize that a 9¢ raise in gas prices is only 2¢ a litre?

Anyway, a vote of confidence on my budget brought down Joe's government that year. But Joe has a short memory, thank the Lord. Why, I'm not even sure if he remembers that I ran against him in 1983. Actually, it's Brian's memory that I have to worry about; I ran against him, too.

It's a high profile job, being Justice Minister, that's for sure. And although we have some pretty strange traditions in this country — such as allowing people to be considered innocent until proven guilty, like that creep journalist who snuck those phony explosives unto that plane — it's still my job to defend those laws, and make sure that they are followed. But then, a lot of people in power have to do unpleasant things, in order to keep their jobs.

I miss Newfoundland, of course; Ottawa really is a pretty dull place. But then, things in our nation's capital are run pretty much like they are in the outports, so I feel right at home, most of the time.

The future? Only time and tide will tell, and back in Newfoundland, we've got plenty of both. But one thing is for darned sure: as long as I hold this Justice portfolio, there will be justice served in this country, even if I have to bend every law in order to do it. I didn't come from That Rock to this Hard Place for nothing.

Just as I was really getting my teeth into the pimps, whores and filth, what happens, but the old boy is zapped from Justice over to Transport. And seeing those dirty movies and magazines was one helluva lot more interesting than watching the trains go by.

Not only that: I'm going to be responsible for the deregulation of airlines, trains, and all that stuff. If you've ever taken the rails in Newfoundland, you'd know how lousy that is.

Then again, I'm really only going from sluts to budget cuts, from porn to airborne, and from trash to train crash. So it's all the same to me. Anyway, there's supposed to be romance in travel, which is more than I was ever able to find in photos of men dancing with sheep, or whatever the hell they were doing.

RAMON HNATYSHYN

As of the summer of 1986, I have been stuck with John Crosbie's Justice portfolio. This might sound boring. But if you could see the books, mags and videotapes inside that portfolio, you'd be as excited as I am!

HOWARD PAWLEY

(Available in English only. If you don't like it,
what are you gonna do about it? Sue?)

"Democracy can be promising," some reporters joked. "Promise-a-Day-Pawley," they mocked. *But look who won.* Mr. Frenchie Bourassa talks big about comebacks, but I've never seen *him* bounce back from trailing the Tories by 30%, to winning a majority like I did back in March of '86.

I merely asked the public to Stand Up for Manitoba, and they did, by God. They voted proudly, confidently, eagerly, for the New Democratic Party of this province, making it the only provincial NDP administration in Canada (not including Ontario, but Peterson won't admit it). And they sent us back into office by flooding us with 41% of the ballots cast.

And I've kept my promises.

I've promised to raise taxes, and I will.

I've promised to freeze the wages of Manitoba teachers — and with our shitty weather, they shouldn't notice the freeze, anyway.

I've promised to be upset by the Feds cutting $50 million off their equalization payments to Manitoba, and boy, *am* I.

I promised not to trust Mulroney, after he shafted our province's Bristol Aerospace and gave that CF-18 jet fighter maintenance contract to Canadair of Montreal, and I *still* don't.

I promised the farmers that they should expect low prices for their crops, and they've gotten them.

I promised that our deficit will run around half a billion, and it has.

I promised that we'd spend 100 million over a decade to clean up the Red and Assiniboine Rivers, and *we will* — I just didn't promise *when* the project will finally begin. Like maybe in the year 2025.

So why aren't the people of Manitoba happy?

For a government with a cash flow as flat as our topography, I'd say I've got a pretty good record, huh?

Why don't they just bitch about the weather? It's all the Tories' fault, anyway.

So let me use this collection of autobiographies to make one more promise: To continue to Stand Up for my province, as we march boldly over no hills or valleys into the very promising future. Marching. Singing. Working together. All in the *one* (1) official language of Canada.

Straight from the Gas

MARCEL MASSE

I have the formula, finally:

$$E = Mc \text{ *}$$

* Energy equals Masse times Coal. Or whatever the public is heating with, nowadays.

Straight from the Used Car Lot

FRANK MILLER

I don't even know why anyone would want to have me in this book, anyway. I'm through with politics, and I'm through with all the heartache, the backstabbing, the tension. Hell, I had a heart attack back in '76, and had threats made on my life, just because I merely wanted to close down a few hundred unnecessary hospitals across Ontario. And then, when I finally won my party's nomination as leader of the Progressive Conservative Party of Ontario in January of 1985 — after nearly every other pinko-Tory politician in the province tried to gang up on me — so what happens? I get trounced by some Yuppie punk, fresh out of kindergarten, whose Gritty party hadn't won an election in over forty years. I get demolished, just because I tried to move the party to the right after years of more waffling than at a convention of Belgian breakfast chefs. No, you won't have Frank Miller to kick around anymore.

Does anyone care that I was the youngest of five, and that my daddy died when I was only 13, leaving us destitute? (You would have thought that, with a background like that, I would have become a socialist, but I was too bright to respond to adversity that way.) Does anyone give a damn that we had to move up to Muskoka, two hours north of Toronto, where my mom actually served as a housekeeper for a distant relative for the next 15 years? A housekeeper!! Is that any sort of job for the mother of a future Tory? I thought we Conservatives were supposed to be rich!

So I slugged it through a chemical engineering course at McGill, worked for a paint-brush manufacturer, taught high school chemistry in Aurora, house-painted in Markham, until I finally moved back up north, where I began to develop resort properties.

I parlayed my properties into over a million clams, while making big bucks from my GM dealership in Bracebridge. (To this day, I have no idea why I was constantly smeared by the press as a "car dealer." I'm an engineer, darn it. I taught school. I've had 50 different jobs in my 59 years, and they try to tar me with the line "used-car salesman." It's just not fair.)

I was elected a Bracebridge town councillor for three years in the late '60s, ran for the mayoralty and lost, and then swept to power along with Bill Davis, in the election of October, 1971. The rest you pretty well know already: Health Minister, '74 to '77. Minister of Natural Resources, ''77 to '78. Minister of Treasury and Economics, '78 to '83. Minister of Industry and Trade, '83 to '85. And then, Premier of Ontario, following Bill Davis's stepping down.

I made some mistakes; I'll admit that. Putting taxes on tampons, for instance. But I had no idea that they were an essential product; I come from a religious background, and we never spoke about unpleasant things like that. And that legislation which ripped up government contracts with its workers was just an attempt to cut down on paperwork.

I could have saved this province, but the public blew it. I would have stopped the stupid demands for bilingualism; allowed the doctors to extra bill all they wanted; given billions more to Ontario Hydro — the best utility on the face of the earth — until they got it right; stopped those filthy videotapes from flooding into Ontario and destroying the moral fibre of our citizens. (If it keeps up at the pace it's going, pornography will probably make every citizen want to use tampons, whether they need them or not.)

As far as Bill Davis's extending the public funding for Catholic schools through grade 12, all I can say is *thank you* Bill. It was certainly a *lovely* gift to leave the man who replaced you as Premier of Ontario and had to call an election within a few months after that. And Bill — the last paragraph is a dictionary definition of sarcasm.

Let's face it, the Tories of Ontario were more Progressive than Conservative. I mean, *really*: Feeding the poor, caring for the sick, helping the elderly. Is this a province, or the Salvation Army that we were running here?

Well, we're running it no longer. The public has spoken. They'll be sorry, but they have spoken, and what they've gotten is two parties for the price of one: Peterson's Grits and Rae's Socialists. I would like to say that politics makes strange bedfellows, except that I don't think those two parties sleeping together is so strange at all.

Anyway, I'm back in Bracebridge now, retired from the dirty world of politics and the city of filthy videotapes. But I'm not retired from my first and greatest love. Which is why I am making this offer to every lucky man and woman who is reading this book: I've got a gorgeous car for you, if you really want a deal. It's a '77 Chevrolet, driven only on Sundays by a little old lady who never shifted out of second gear and always voted for the Ontario Tories, which is the same thing. The cost? It's too low for me to have it printed in this book. Just give me a call, at Area Code 705, USED-CAR. That's 705, U-S-E-D-C-A-R. The colour is a bit grotesque — tartan — but it's a real steal. Call me today, before the Grits and Socialists take away the last bit of cash you have, and blow it on Suncor, or something idiotic like that.

Put down this book and pick up that phone. You won't regret it. Have I ever lied to you before?

Straight from Whatever Colour Peril It Is This Week

GERRY WEINER

Tamils. Turks. I never knew such people even *existed*. Life was so much easier as a pharmacist; as Minister of Immigration, I don't push pills; they push *me*.

Why don't they all go back where they *came* from?*

* Hold on a minute. How soon can these guys *vote*?

67

ROBERT BOURASSA

They talk of comebacks in sports. They talk of comebacks in religion — Lazarus had a good one. But when future generations talk of comebacks in politics, they will surely talk of me, Robert Bourassa, as the greatest comebacker in history. To have won the premiership of the province of Quebec in 1970, and again in 1973, and then to be in the wilderness for nearly a decade, and then to win the premiership once again in 1986, is surely one of the most *magnifique* comebacks of all time. And I did this all without being friends with Pierre Trudeau.

I once described myself as "the last chance for Quebec," since, as everyone knew, *après moi, les séparatistes*. Well, the séparatistes have come and gone, and I'm still here, am I not? So it looks as if my wonderful province has given me one last chance, and I do not plan to blow it this time, let me tell you. I still have nervous hair, but it is not so nervous that I will have my hairdresser on staff anymore, *bien sûr*.

The youngest prime minister in the history of the province of Quebec — *c'est moi* — was born in the summer of 1933, the only child of Aubert and Adrienne (Courville) Bourassa, in Montreal, a town west of Quebec City, the capital, where I would eventually become such a force for good. Being an only child can be lonely, but it allowed me to tell everyone that my much older brother was Henri Bourassa, the great journalist and nationalist. To be fair, we are both descended from the same settlers of Quebec, two centuries ago. So there. My father was a bookkeeper in the federal civil service, which made me realize at a young age that there was a good living to be made, if you were willing to play ball with Ottawa.

My father died when I was a teenager, leaving my mother and me a lot less well-off than wealthy Québécois like Mr. Trudeau. But I was such a brilliant student, I began to win scholarships by the dozens, allowing me to get a very good education at very low prices. I earned extra Canadian dollars by delivering groceries, and they were worth more than American bucks at that time, which was before Trudeau destroyed our country's economy.

I earned my BA from Jean-de-Brébeuf College, which was a remarkable foreshadowing; Brébeuf was martyred by the Iroquois in 1649; I wasn't martyred until 1976, and then it was by the Parti Québécois. I then graduated with my law degree from the University of Montreal in 1956. I won the Governor General's Medal as the highest-ranking member of my class. Just think of it! The Governor General's medal! And if we had followed the evil P.Q., they would have had such wonderful honours eliminated! Can you blame me for being such a strong federalist??

I was admitted to the Quebec bar in 1957, and, having won a Rhodes scholarship — I told you I was bright, did I not? — I attended Oxford University in England, where I earned my MA in economics in 1959. My thesis was on the role of crown corporations in the Canadian economy. Then, in 1959-60, I went to the United States, where I was supported by scholarships from the Mackenzie King Foundation, the Royal Society of Canada, and the Ford Foundation. I began to feel that I would never have to support myself again. I eventually earned another MA in international tax and corporate law from Harvard University. I was certainly a lot more educated than Mr. Lévesque, with his crummy BA.

By 1960, I had had enough of schooling, and I wanted to be where the action was: Ottawa. I became a legal advisor in the Department of National Revenue in our nation's capital for the next three years, bringing cases against business firms which had evaded their taxes. Whew. And you think I was hated when I was premier of Quebec!

From 1963 to 1965, I was the research director of the Belanger Royal Commission on Public Finances in Quebec, for which I prepared a major report on my province's tax structure. Not only did this make me intimate with Quebec finances but my name and excellence became known to Jean Lesage, the Liberal Premier of Quebec at the time. By 1966, he had the intelligence to recruit me as a Liberal candidate for a seat in the Quebec National Assembly. It was actually called the Legislative Assembly at that time, but who remembers? Hell, I was once the most despised man in all of Quebec, and who remembers?

It was the Mercier riding, which included my home, and Lesage was kind enough to appoint the incumbent to a judgeship, to make room for me. Politics is like that; you have to admire its pragmatism.

Alors, the provincial election of 1966 was not a happy one for the Liberals; Lesage was forced to give up the premiership, but remained party leader, as we lost our majority to the wretched Union Nationale. But enough of the party; what about me? Ahh, I was welcomed with great passion. "A new style politician!" they called me in the press. "A cool technocrat," they called me, at a time when everybody knew that to be cool was to be with it.

I was a smashing success, overwhelming my opponent by a crushing 518 votes in the balloting. Lesage promptly made me the finance critic in the Assembly, president of the Liberal party's political commission, and a member of its strategy committee. All this at the age of 33, when even Jesus Christ was on his way out. At the same time, I taught public finance at Laval and Montreal Universities; a man has to make a living, you know.

Not that I had to make that much of a living, to be honest. You see, back in 1958, I married my beautiful wife Andrée Simard. Her father was Joseph Edouard Simard, a rather successful businessman in my province. The realization that Andrée, our two children and myself would never starve was a great source of strength to me, during my political career; I recommend it to all my friends.

Then, in September, 1968, a Great Opportunity Came Knocking; how wonderful that I was standing near the door at the time: Jean Lesage announced that he was retiring. Nearly three dozen senior Liberals formed the Committee of the Friends of Robert Bourassa, to push for my candidacy. And why not? I had been a backbencher for more than three years, by that time. I had waited long enough to make my move.

Lesage remained neutral, but he kept throwing speaking engagements my way, which suggested his support. A very special poll took place that fall, which showed that nearly one-half of the voters of Quebec did not know who the hell I was, but this did not sadden me. I knew that the less they knew about me, the less they would hate me. And history has proven me correct.

I had everything the voters would want: I was handsome — and this was even before my hairdresser came on board, I want you to know; I had a beautiful wife; I had a very wealthy father-in-law; I had been in politics so little time that my opponents could not smear me with association with Lesage's government; and I was *très expert* in financial matters, so the voters knew that even if things did not work out, I could always do their income tax for them. I use H. & R. Block, myself.

In January, 1970, at our party's leadership convention at the Quebec Coliseum, I was chosen party leader by the 1550 delegates. They made a very wise decision indeed.

In the election of April 29, 1970, my party had gained 72 of the 108 seats in the Assembly, which was a great victory for me and the Quebec Liberals. We had won only 45% of the vote, however, which I'd rather not talk about. Levesque's Péquistes, on the other hand, had only 7 seats, which was laughable. They also had nearly one-quarter of all the votes, which was enough to weep. As *Maclean's* noted that summer, "Bourassa's victory was not a definite yes or no to federalism — at most it was a resolute maybe." So what's wrong with that? Without maybes, resolute or otherwise, where would most politicians be?

I took office on May 12, 1970, as the youngest premier in my province's history. I know that I said that in the third paragraph, but I like to talk about it. Since I knew more about finance than anyone else in the province, I took over the Finance portfolio at the same time. And since I knew more about other governments than anyone else in the province, I took over the portfolio of Intergovernmental Affairs, as well. Come to think of it, I really didn't need any Cabinet at all. I have always considered it a weakness to have to delegate authority; I am sure that you readers will agree with me on that.

Less than half a year after I took office as Premier of Quebec, there was that stupid brouhaha with the FLQ, which so disrupted our lives, not to mention that of Pierre LaPorte, who was my Labour Minister. I was masterful in the situation, ordering Prime Minister Trudeau to invoke the War Measures Act, even though there are few Japanese in Quebec. Pierre reluctantly went along, fearful that he was, but it was a great, great success. The FLQ was destroyed more or less painlessly. OK, so we lost our civil liberties for awhile! Over 90% of Québécois agreed with me, and my government was never stronger. And we got back our snooty habeas corpus and stuff like that in just a few weeks, anyway.

Then, less than a year later, another crisis! (Richard Nixon had six big ones, as I remember, and look well how he ended up). There was a silly little meeting with all the premiers in Victoria, in the summer of 1971, and I agreed to drop those stupid demands our province has always made about autonomy. But when I got back to Quebec, what a big deal! A lot of my Cabinet Ministers — I told you that I really didn't need them — had begun an anti-charter campaign.

But why fight when you can switch. I simply changed my mind and told Pierre that I was now rejecting the charter. I told him that it wasn't clear on whether my province could run its own social welfare measures or not. Boy, the Anglos were pissed off! But I had come out on top, again!

In the meantime, I was simply magnificent as premier of Quebec. I opened our first steel plant in 1972, showing the greatness of our province. And I pushed for the mammoth James Bay hydroelectric project, in spite of petty, selfish complaints from such uninvolved troublemakers as local Indians, childish environmentalists, and others. I also became famous for creating an astounding number of new jobs in the province — at least 55,000 — earning me the honourable label of "Bob-la-Job."

I ran the province like a top, surrounding myself with a half-dozen geniuses, known affectionately as *"les maudits whiz kids."* By using frequent private opinion polls — often as many as two or three a day — I was able to keep up with the attitudes and opinions of the citizens of the province. (My friend Bill Davis, in neighbouring Ontario, picked up this idea from me.)

In the next provincial elections, in the fall of 1973, I achieved a glorious victory. The Liberals captured 102 of the 110 seats in the National Assembly, with 54% of the vote. Not bad. The malignant PQ lost one of its seven seats, in spite of increasing its share of the popular vote to nearly one-third of the populace. How's that for representation, eh?

In my second term in office, I was even more superb, making me wonder all the more why they turfed me out in '76. I made French the official language of Quebec with Bill 22, which was loved by everyone except the Anglos, other minority groups, and even the PQ, who couldn't seem to be satisfied with anything. Trudeau wasn't too happy, either, but why should he have been so irritable? Couldn't he understand that I had to sit in front of an opposition every day which wanted to make Quebec an independent country? He didn't have to face that. So what did he do? He called me

"*Ti-pit*," which means small boy, when I'm really quite big for my age.

Even labour was hard on me, when I've always been so sympathetic to them. They didn't appreciate my anti-strike law, which I pushed through in early 1976, and they were put off by my jailing their leaders to break a general strike, back in 1972. But I was pro-labour, I swear! If it weren't for workers, how on earth could we raise the taxes that we need to support our government?

And so it came: The day that will live in infamy. On November 15, 1976, I lost both my seat in the National Assembly, and the premiership. What a thankless people! Did I not find jobs for hairdressers; for media experts, who always made sure that only my best side would be captured in photographs; for hundreds of cronies who might not have found gainful employment outside of government?

Did they not know that I am buddy-buddy with the Rockefellers? Did they want to be *maîtres chez nous*, or not? So they said that I was lacking in emotion; did they want Johnny Ray? So they said that I looked stiff; some men would pay millions to look stiff, even only occasionally.

Hell, it was I who created The Greatest Project of the Quiet Revolution, the James Bay Project! So the cost rose from $5.8 billion to nearly three times that; big deal. Drapeau did the same with the Olympics, and everyone loved it.

But enough of cavilling; I lost, and that was that. Did I sit around and sulk? Not on your hairdresser, I didn't. I went off to Belgium, France and the United States to sulk, leaving the wife and kids back in Montreal.

I was hardly forgotten, of course. Fond memories of my inspired leadership were on most Quebeckers' minds, as Lévesque and the PQ drove the province to near-ruin. For instance, my good friend Claude Ryan, said, in 1979, "Bourassa should abstain from politics for at least ten years." It was kind of him to suggest that I needed such a long rest, after all my hard work on behalf of Quebec, but I was prepared to return much earlier.

At the age of 50, I replaced Ryan as leader of my beloved party once more. They could hardly wait to have me back, and who could blame them? True, I passed up a few by-elections, rather than run for the Assembly, but with a guy who has a great name like Gérard

D. Lévesque to run things in Quebec City, I didn't feel that I had to. The people were totally confused.

When the election finally came, in early 1986, my Liberals wiped the floor with the Separatistes. Of course, we lacked a party with such exciting members as Gilles Grégoire and Claude Charron, but somehow, we managed. And the people in my riding were so excited to have me back, they gave me a second chance to run, in another riding, so others could also have the thrill and honour of voting for me.

Have I changed? On the important things, *bien sûr*. The hairdresser is long gone. My horned-rimmed glasses have given away to a lighter-coloured pair.

But in minor ways, I'm still the same old lovable Robert: I still have no interests outside politics; I still do exactly 20 lengths in a pool every day; I still sleep seven hours every night, to the minute; I still hate Trudeau's guts.

You know, a week is a long time in politics, and a year is an eternity. So imagine how long it's been for me, to be out of power for a full decade. Still, time changes nearly everything. Why, when I was last in power, John Turner was in exile in Toronto; now he's in exile in Ottawa. When I was last in power, Brian Mulroney was just a lackey on the Cliche commission; today, he's a lackey for the United States. But they are both my close friends, in spite of their flaws. When I was last in power, Pierre Elliott Trudeau was the Prime Minister of Canada. I'm not sure what the hell ever happened to him.

And *moi*? I am, once again, the Premier of Quebec. You can go home again, even if you've got to comb your own hair, this time around.

MARTIN GOLDFARB

Answer each of these questions, please:

1. Did you vote in the last federal election, in September, 1984?
2. If so, did you vote PC, NDP, Liberal, or other?
3. If an election were held today, for which national party would you vote?

Thanks. Fill in the above, and send it off to Angus Reid. I've run this country too damned long, and I'm tired. It's a dirty job; let somebody else do it.

IONA CAMPAGNOLA

Dedicated to the Greatest Prime Minister, the Greatest
Man Who Ever Walked the Face of the Earth: Pierre Trudeau

They call me aloof. They call me brittle. They call me cold. Me,
cold? Hah. Ever been in Winnipeg in February? What they should
call me is Iona, since that is what I answer to, although a call for
Renewal, Reform and Review of the Federal Liberal Party will get
my attention as well. After all, I'm Iona Campagnola, the first female
president of the Liberal Party of Canada, the party which saved
this country in this century, and which will save the country in
the next, if only the populace will wake up and smell the burning
coffee, toast and bridges of the Tories.

Since I'm used to making two or three major speeches a day, all
different, in two or three different provinces or territories, it wasn't
hard to sit down and dash off an autobiography. After all, there
was a one-hour stop between planes in Glace Bay, where I am sitting now, in an airport hanger. But when you work for something
you believe in — and I believe in the Liberal Party, that's for sure,
more than God Herself — you can find time for anything. Except
maybe human relationships, which aren't my bag, anyway.

I was born Iona Hardy in the Gulf Islands of British Columbia,
to a fishing family, the oldest of four children. Even before I
pubesced — and I did that beautifully, you should know — I was
working on the cannery line on the Skeena Slough each summer.
You might think I smelled of fish, but it was nothing, compared
to the stinking reek of the Tuna Scandal of the Tories in 1985. Yes,
even as a child, I was as partisan as all getout.

My clothes were ordered from Simpsons' and Eatons' catalogues,
and it was almost impossible to get the right colour. I always in-
sisted on wearing all red, a prescient suggestion of my future political
leanings.

As a child, I was always told that this thing couldn't be done,
or that thing couldn't be done. How typically Canadian! I've always
believed that, if you work hard enough, you can do anything you

want to do. Of course, kicking out 211 incompetent Tory Members of Parliament in the mid-1980s might take a bit longer, that's all. But you just wait.

In my 20s, I married a Skeena fisherman and stayed at home with my two beautiful, brainy and Liberal daughters. But I slowly began to ask myself, "Is That All There Is?" In fact, I asked myself that question so much, when Peggy Lee came out with that hit song, I tried to sue her for plagiarism. I lost the case, but gained solace from having Betty Friedan quoting me over eight dozen times in *The Feminine Mystique*. God, but I hated being a housewife!

So I made a decision: I would be a loner and strike out on my own, a drifter, alone, rootless. (That's *rootless*, not *ruthless*. The latter refers to Conservatives.) I gave up men, in a kind of life-long Lent, and began to move out into the wider world. And, let me tell you, once you get out of Skeena, almost any place on earth is the Big Time. Hell, Prince Rupert was New York City, after Skeena.

I struggled, I fought, I debated, I raged, I clawed, and I finally made it: I became the President of the Prince Rupert Garden Club. (Don't laugh. Those ladies fight dirty.) In 1966, I ran for school board trustee in that gigantic metropolis, then for chairperson of the school board, and eventually alderperson. But did I stop? No-ma'am-ree. I had promises to keep, and kilometres to go before I sleep. (Yes, we Liberals are *all* for metric, and *proudly* so.)

By 1974, I was working at a local television station as a test pattern — there's really nothing to do up in northern British Columbia — when I won the Liberal nomination in the Skeena riding. I stunned the world, or at least the hundreds of Skeena voters, by demolishing the 17-year incumbent of the New Democratic Party. It was one of the best election victories the Liberals had ever won in the West, and it was Iona Campagnola who had done it. And no one would forget it. *I wouldn't let them.*

I took Ottawa by storm. True, they were used to lousy weather in that tedious town, but I was a grand success. I was parliamentary secretary to Judd Buchanan, who was then Minister of Indian and Northern Affairs — women can speak with forked tongue, too — and then I finally got named to my own ministry: Fitness and Amateur Sport. And why not? I was fit, and an amateur, and a good sport — you have to be, to be a woman in federal Liberal politics — and besides, I had three qualifications which the Liberal party

77

needed badly and lacked horribly. No, not breasts and a womb, although you're getting warm: I was a Woman, a Westerner, and a Northerner. Who could ask for anything more?

Pierre Elliott Trudeau, the genius, the giant, the god, had dared me to do something in a field which had been usually dominated by persons of the hairier, flat-chested persuasion. I was no hot-house flower; I took a crummy little portfolio and made it into something great.

In the meantime, I fought valiantly for the citizens of my riding, which happened to be the second biggest one in the country — in size, not in population. For instance, in 1976, there was $26 million given in LIP grants to 23 ridings in British Columbia. But the good people of Skeena, my riding, received $2.7 million. I'm told that this is legal.

Anyway, guess how they thanked me for all my help? I was bounced out by the NDP in the 1979 election. That's the last time I'll try to buy votes; it never seems to work. To be fair — something that the Tories would never understand — there was something else that worked against me: the federal government had cut subsidies to a water transportation system that had served a lot of the outports in Skeena, and that really undermined me. I fought to have the decision changed, but no go. It sure is tough to be a Woman, a Westerner and a Northerner, even though I really thought the federal Liberals were so pleased to have all three in one such perfect body. Boy, did I give the BC party establishment hell. And hell hath no fury, etc.

So there I was. It was 1979. I was a single parent and a former MP. What else could I do? I moved back to British Columbia, where I hosted an interview show in Vancouver for the CBC, of blessed memory (the Corporation, not the show), and I set up a fundraising organization called Ionasphere Management Corporation. Cute title, eh? I consulted for various groups like CUSO, who wanted me to help raise funds for a refugee camp in Thailand. (The homeless in Canada didn't appear until the Tories came to power in '84.)

But my exile from politics was soon to end. After two years of hosting that TV show, *One of a Kind* — a good description of me, huh? — I had to leave the job when the CBC developed a policy which disallowed recent politicians to work for them. Damn them.

I was angry. Angry at the world. And especially at the BC Liberals,

78

who had been out of power for so long, they had forgotten what steak tartar, pomme frites and Chateau Reichmann 1891 (a good year) tasted like. When they had the unmitigated gall to approach me to be their provincial leader, I tore them to shreds. I told them they had a vested interest in defeat, and that really got their goat. Actually, the BC Liberals had given up the goat many years before.

Well, to tell the truth, I was suffering from "the spotlight syndrome," as the campaign manager of my fight for the federal Liberal presidency puts it. I needed to be where the action was. My party was in trouble, although I had no idea why; did not Pierre Elliott Trudeau, God Bless Him, do Glories and Wonders for this country almost non-stop since 1968? But somehow or other, our federal party had appeared to lose touch with the West. Indeed, Liberal MPs from west of Kenora were as scarce as hen's teeth. To be blunt, Liberal MPs from west of Kenora were as scarce as Aquino supporters at a Ferdinand and Imelda bash. Something had to be done!

That something was Iona Campagnolo. *Moi.* I was reluctant to run for the post at first, since the pay was so lousy: less than 25 grand a year. But I knew that I could change that quickly, which I did. Within three months, I managed to get through a 140% pay hike, bringing me up to what a Cabinet minister would get for doing a hellova lot less; around 60 Gs. Talk about equal pay for work of equal value, huh?

I took on my predecessor, Norman MacLeod, and washed the floor with him — a woman's work is never done — beating him by a margin of two to one. There *had* been some dirty tricks; some tears; some mud-slinging; a few dead and wounded. But nothing more than you might expect at a Progressive Conservative caucus meeting on an average day.

I took over the presidency of the federal Liberal Party in November, 1982, and I ran it perfectly until I stepped down in 1986. True, we had a slight setback in September, 1984 — Brian the Phony would still be chasing ambulances in Baie Comeau, if they had chosen me instead of Turner — but we're on the way back. You'll see.

The future? A Liberal-run Canada into the 23rd century. A Senate seat for me, or at least a winnable MP seat in the West, which involves having to run an election, alas. After all, I've always said that I wanted to spend my second half-century working in the Third

World. And with the way the Tories are dismantling the Canadian economy, I may never have to leave home at all. And let's face it: Someone with the body, hair and cheekbones I've got will always rise to the top, no matter where she is.

BILL BENNETT

Kelowna. As in clown-a. That's the Bethlehem of British Columbia politics, at least since 1952, when God the Father began to run
our most beautiful province. (And it's true; I've seen that line on
lots of license plates out here). I've run it, as the world knows so
well, because of Expo 86, since 1975. And now, at the peak of my
career, I've chosen to step down. But then, what's wrong with that?
If Trudeau had done that, back in 1971, this country might still have
had a chance.

My Dad was W.A.C. Bennett, of course, who had been raised
in Poverty, a small town in New Brunswick, which is a province
somewhere to the east of the prairies. At the age of 30, he brought
my mom and two older siblings to this blessed province, where he
purchased a small hardware store. Not unlike Jesus's father, if I
recall.

In 1936, Dad tried for a provincial Tory nomination and lost, but
within five years, that old party saw the light, and he was elected
MLA for South Okanagan in 1941. Who knew then that it was the
start of a great Dynasty of Bennetts? As opposed to the Dynasty
of the Colbys, of course, who are not as wealthy as we are.

It was hell, growing up in the Okanagan Valley. No, not because
my Dad didn't become a millionaire for a number of years — that
was rough, too. No, it was because I had terrible allergies, and the
Valley has got a pollen count higher than the number of penny
stocks on the V.S.E. When I was six, Daddy took me to a national
Conservative convention in Ottawa, and I knew immediately what
would take most boys my age many, many years to discover: there
is far less pollen in the area of the nation's capital. But that's still
no reason to want to move there, as most any MP will tell you. And
as any Ontario license plate will also tell you, that province is not
the most beautiful one.

My Dad taught me invaluable lessons about thrift and hard work,
especially when I got to see him on his trips home from Victoria,
which were about once a year. I'd have to chop wood, pile it up,
clean the stairs, and take out the garbage, or else I wouldn't get
an allowance. And today, in British Columbia, we demand the same

81

of our welfare recipients, who now number about a third of the populace.

In fact, the Bennett family had a rule: when each of the kids turned 13, he had to go out and get a job. I've tried to make this a revered family tradition for all British Columbians, but most of the jobs seem to be in other provinces, so the 13-year-olds keep heading east.

My Dad switched from the Conservative party to the Social Credit party in 1951, and became Premier of British Columbia in 1952. By that time, he had turned our tiny hardware store into a multi-million dollar conglomerate, which just goes to show how well a man can do, when he's got friends in high places. And in more than one political party, too! That's really what capitalism is all about, and I had hoped to instill that kind of frontier spirit in the province before I left office.

Then, in September, 1973, after my Dad stepped down from the Premiership — it was about time!! — I made my Big Move, and won his seat in a by-election. That's spelled "by-election," *not* "buy-election"; this ain't the Phillipines. The fact that we had the same last name had no effect on my nomination and election, of course, any more than Bobby or Teddy Kennedy's last name did on their political careers. But it probably didn't hurt, either. *The Vancouver Province*, between strikes at the time, called my entry into politics "a new lease on death" for the Socreds, which I'm still trying to figure out.

Anyway, the NDP ran the province into the ground from 1972 to 1975, but the Natural Order was restored in 1975, 1979, and 1983. I quickly moved into an apartment-hotel next door to the legislature in Victoria, which shocked many people, but I got a *great* deal on the rent, until I removed controls some years later. It's true, I left my wonderful family behind in Kelowna, but then, hundreds of thousands of British Columbians have been forced to leave their homes, too, so I'm not so different from them.

And I am proud of what I've done for this blessed province: I withheld cost-of-living increases to the handicapped; abolished rent control; abolished the Human Rights Commission (as Barry Goldwater once wisely said, "No law can make you like me or me like you"); and eliminated death duties and gift taxes on the fortunes of the deceased wealthy.

82

It's a thankless job, being a premier. Sometimes, I feel that the only British Columbians who haven't viciously attacked me are the Doukhobors. But then, most of them didn't have clothes before I came to power, anyway, so what have they lost under me?

I'm just a highly-disciplined person with strong personal work habits and dedication. I don't drink and I don't smoke, and I see no reason why my fellow citizens of this province should have any fun, either. "Restraint" is said to be my middle name, but it's really not so. It's "Closure." I've made sure that civil servants *leave* their jobs the exact same way that they *came* to them: fired with enthusiasm. (A little levity, there.)

Look, for nearly a dozen years, I had the greatest job in British Columbia. In fact, in Canada. And with all the terrible unemployment around this province, most people didn't expect me to give it up. I used to tell my fellow citizens: if you've got a job, hang onto it for all it's worth. But a man gets tired; there comes a point when you've had enough. True, my boys are still a bit young to take over. But my father made me sweat; let them sweat a bit too.

So I've decided to step down, and when I make a decision, it's settled. I was in power when Expo 86 took place, and that's good enough for me. I even got to meet Princess Di and that man with her. No, I'm off to relax in Kelowna for the next few decades, and maybe pick up some $10,000-a-day jobs on a few dozen major business boards, just like Peter Lougheed. Dad and I ran this province almost non-stop since 1952, and you can see by the thousands of happy people in the streets, many of them in hot pants and garter belts, we did a knock-out job.

Straight from the Seeing-eye Trust

SINCLAIR STEVENS

I want to be left a loan.

MICHEL COGGER

So I'm in the Senate. So what. Lots of people are in the Canadian Senate. Why point *me* out?

Hell, it's not patronage; not at all. Unlike most of the lackeys and cronies and hangers-on that the Grits kept choosing for the Senate, over the past two decades, I've got quite a number of qualifications. Such as:

— I was a buddy of Brian Mulroney, back in Laval Law.

— I was Brian Mulroney's personal lawyer for a number of years.

— I was the best man at the wedding of Brian and Mila.

— I was the funnel for a $25,000 donation to Brian's campaign against Joe Clark, back in 1983, that Walter Wolf provided, to assist Brian in his race for Tory leader.

— There was only one Quebec vacancy open for the Senate, and I'm from Montreal.

Now, what could make me more qualified for the Senate than that?

Straight from the Rock (and Don't Knock It, Either)

BRIAN PECKFORD

Dearrrrrrrr Mr. Stoddarrrrrrrd:

Aye appreciates yur note, requestin' me writing me life story fur yur anthulogy, *Straight from the Lip*, which me gathers will appearrrr this yarrrrr. Aye woold luv ta rite me autobiography, since Aye have such a trrilling tale ta tell ya, me b'y. I wuz an Ainglesh teacher fur awile, and I'da luved to be poobleshed. But th' fact is, Ayze bean cawt up in soom yoonion prublems out here in Newfoundland, as well as been French-fried by them dolts in Ottawa, so Ayze decided to jes' brrrriefly annsur sum of yur kwestyons:

1. It's harder, but yes, I'll write this in English, rather than my native tongue. I'll have it translated before I send it in.

2. No, I am not the *only* person who hasn't left Newfoundland for Boston, but, on the other hand, there is some truth to the accusation that we haven't been growing terribly much as a province. But I am out to make it possible so that all those who have left the Rock — around seven million, at last count — will be able to come back, find jobs, and live here happily ever after, like the many thousands who live here now still do.

3. I was born in a small outport, Whitbourne, in 1942. My dad was a welfare officer for the provincial government. Coincidentally, we've got lots on welfare today. But that's another matter.

4. I have absolutely no recollections of Newfoundland joining Confederation, except for a lot of noise. Today, I realize that the sounds were just people leaving for New England in large numbers. Joey — the original Newfie — told us that Confederation would mean manna from heaven, and in a way, he was correct. Today, federal transfers of cash and other government spending make up four-fifths of the provincial cash flow. I'm not too hots for Ottawa, and I just *hate* Toronto — but then *everyone* feels the same way as I do, about that burg — yet I know that we'd starve to death if it weren't for those bastards. Cod damn them.

5. I taught high school English from 1966 to 1972. It was fun, because in Newfoundland, *all* English teaching is E.S.L. (English as a Second Language).

6. In 1972, when we finally dumped the Only Living Father, and Frank Moores took office, the Green Bay riding went Tory for the first time in its history. I was the winner, at the age of 29. We prodigies work that way.

7. I served in the municipal affairs and housing portfolio in Moores' cabinet from 1974 on, and succeeded him as PC leader in 1979. I was tough with Ottawa, fighting the cretins over off-shore rights, and was soon called "Confederation's Bad Boy." Cod almighty, who is the "bad" one in all this? I mean, after getting ripped off by Hydro-Quebec over the Churchill Falls development in Labrador, can you blame me for not trusting anyone? Cod damn them all.

8. Yes, that includes my ex-wife, and it's none of your goddam business, either.

9. I've won three electoral victories, and could win the next three, if I so choose. Whether the people will so choose is another matter. Cod bless 'em all.

10. Yes, we have nothing but the biggest and the best in my province: the highest sales tax in Canada (12%); the highest cost of living in Canada; the highest unemployment (over 20%). We also have the largest emigration, which is always opening up valuable new jobs.

11. I was the brilliant mind behind the Atlantic Accord with Ottawa in 1985, when the Feds agreed to share management and revenues from all Newfoundland offshore resource development. Churchill Falls will be revenged, yet. Of course, in retrospect, I should have included fish along with the oil.

12. I spent nearly half a million in renovating my offices on the eighth floor of the Confederation Building in St. John's back in 1985. How we managed to do that, when we are so financially strapped, just proves how inspired we are, as the reigning political party of the province. We know our priorities.

13. It's true; I *am* the most organized politician in the entire country. For example, my schedule for one day last January:

7 a.m. Rise and Shine!

8 a.m. Snare rabbits (note: when at my hunting shack on the northeast coast; if in St. John's, it's snare Grits and NDPers, with the latter more numerous recently).

9:15. Pee Pee.

9:17. Hate hour against Toronto, alone in office.

10:17. Hate hour against Ottawa, with advisors.

11:17. Write poison-pen letters to Fraser March of NAPE.

12:00. Hate hour against France, including reading of history texts on Vichy France and the collapse of the Maginot Line.

1:00. Fly to pro football game, preferably on the west coast of the States. Special meal of cod on board.

8:00. Return to St. John's. Work hard on un-learning French.

9:00. Jig for codfish — thems that are left.

10:00. Study Colbys and/or J.R. Ewing on TV for ideas on how to handle labour, opposition parties, and federal PCs in Ottawa.

11:00. Number 2, combined with a few minutes of hate against Leo Barry.

14. That's all from me. I think you've got enough. But before I return to my Confrontation of the Day, I'd just like to inform you that I've got a great deal for you on a zinc mine at Daniel's Harbour. What do you say?

Straight from Ever-So-Slightly Left of Centre

ED BROADBENT

Power corrupts, and absolute power corrupts absolutely. Unfortunately, being the leader of the federal New Democratic party means not having to worry much about that.

Still, it's been a lot of fun, coming in third for the last dozen years. Hell, in the Olympics, coming in third gets you a medal; don't forget that. In many ways, I am a typical "ordinary Canadian," as I like to call my constituents: a Ph.D. in political science; a former university professor; a student of Camus. Well, I have at least *one* thing in common with ordinary Canadians; I can't speak French worth a damn.

I was born John Edward Broadbent — I took my middle name, since it seemed more centralist — in Oshawa, an industrial town just east of Toronto, dominated by the factories of General Motors. My father Percy worked as a clerk in the office of GM. And, as we all know, what's good for General Motors is good for Canada. Or something like that.

I was the second of three children, the first son, and I kept winning all the student awards for brightest kid, even winning enough *Oshawa Times* delivery contests to win a bike. This was long before I learned that incentive is bad for you.

Then, like all working class kids, I won a full scholarship to Trinity College at the University of Toronto. Everyone there was upperclass white Anglo-Saxon Protestant. I was white, Protestant and Anglo-Saxon. Close, but not close enough.

While at U. of T., my political thinking was influenced by Kant, Hegel and Wittgenstein, three early Canadian socialist leaders. I graduated first in my class, took a Masters in Philosophy of Law on a fellowship, and then went off to the London School of Economics on another fellowship, where I took my doctorate in political science. Just an ordinary intellectual. But then, Trudeau was an intellectual too, and he ran the country for a century. Or that's what it felt like.

By 1968, I was feeling restless just teaching political science at York. I decided to stand as a New Democratic party candidate in that year's election, in my old home riding of Oshawa-Whitby.

It was the year of Trudeaulunacy, as everyone calls it nowadays, but I still managed to squeeze past a long-time Oshawa MP who had been the labour minister under Diefenbaker. What a Tory had been doing, representing a factory town, I have no idea. Anyway, I beat him by 15 votes, earning me the title of "Landslide Ed."

Now I was a backbencher, which was pretty tedious, but still a lot better than having to mark all those damned poli sci papers. I helped draft the famed Waffle manifesto, even coining the phrase, "If we must waffle, let us waffle to the left."

In 1971, Tommy Douglas, of blessed memory, stepped down, and I made a wild run for the leadership of the NDP. I say a "wild run," because I wasn't quite sure which way I was going. I quickly learned the dangers of being in the middle; with Jim Laxer's Waffles on the left, and David Lewis's Eggheads on the right, I didn't have a chance. I finished fourth, which was pretty amazing, since there were only two other guys in the race.

No, it hasn't been easy with this party. As John Stuart Mill, my hero, once wrote, "It's my party, and I'll die if I want to." And die I did. Because after David Lewis ran this country from 1972 to 1974, with slight assistance from Pierre Trudeau, we were thrown out of power, and our number of party seats decimated, in July of 1974. Lewis resigned, having lost his seat, and I was appointed interim leader.

It was extremely flattering at first, until I realized that there was no one else around to do the job. Then they really cut me to the quick: Some big shots like then-Manitoba Premier Ed Schreyer — they still haven't found his body in Australia, or wherever the hell he's been banished to — tried to cut me out, by urging Eric Kierans to take the job!

I pulled out of the race, since my feelings were deeply hurt, but stepped back in a few months later, when they still couldn't find anybody who wanted the job. Talk about thankless.

So here I was, backed by David Lewis, Tommy Douglas, Dave Barrett, Alan Blakeney, and even Ed Schreyer (that one took a bit more time), and even then it took to the fourth ballot. And if my opponent hadn't been a woman and a black, I'd probably be teaching Political Science 101 at York University today.

Well, that was July of 1975, and I've done masterfully since then, leading my party to a solid third place victory in 1979, then another strong third place victory in 1980, and, most recently, a stunning third place showing in 1984. What more could the average Canadian want?

I have dedicated my life to the common citizens of this country. I know that they care deeply about unemployment, our economy, the unrestrained power of corporations, the need for a strong labour and trade union movement, consumer and environmental protection, and so on. The New Democratic Party has become the conscience of Parliament, even if our rhetoric sometimes renders most MPs unconscious.

My voice has been described as shrill, but have you ever listened to Sheila Copps? And as for being too intellectual for the average Canadian, surely we underestimate him or her. If given the chance, most citizens of this great land would eagerly read John Stuart Mill; listen to Bartok; vote NDP. We just have to keep plugging away, just like we've been doing all along.

I've often said that if I believed in hell it would consist of New Democrats who spend all eternity selling tickets for fundraising drives to each other. Which reminds me: if any readers of this autobiography are interested, send $5 to me, Ed Broadbent, Parliament Hill, Ottawa, Ontario. You won't regret it. Thousands of ordinary Canadians, like you and me, have done the same.

Straight from The Hangman

WILLIAM DOMM*

I wuz robbed. They *promised* that they'd hold a free vote on my private bill, calling for the dealth penalty. They *promised*. And then, just as suddenly as I had introduced my bill, they somehow managed to withdraw it. It took ages until they finally began debating it. I could *kill* them for that.

* It's spelled D-o-m-m, not D-u-m-b. You abolitionists make me *sick*. I hope you all hang.

Straight from Tunagate

JOHN FRASER

Do you read the lot numbers stamped on the tops of tin cans? Neither do I. So what's the big deal?

Do you watch *the fifth estate* on TV every week? Neither do I. So what's the big deal? Although, I have to admit, I sure am glad that we Tories have been chopping away at the CBC budget.

Does your heart bleed for the starving Ethiopians? Mine too. So why on earth did they prevent Star-Kist from sending some of the tuna to that famine-stricken country? Maybe it was unfit for human consumption, but everyone agrees that the suffering in Ethiopia is positively *in*human, don't they?

What's done is done. Over a million cans of tuna were recalled —Detroit does it with cars, every other week, and who bitches?— and I got dropped from my Federal Fisheries Ministry post.

But it wasn't my fault! Star-Kist Canada Inc. is a subsidiary of H.J. Heinz Co. of Pittsburgh, so it's not even a Canadian company. And no one really got sick from that tuna. Except me.

Those lot numbers? Bye the Sea, Lot No. 629VFBS159, and Star-Kist Lot No. 949VCB233. Try them in a lottery, sometime. At least someone should come out of this thing smelling like a winner.

Straight from the Fish's (and Speaker's) Mouth:

JOHN FRASER, *again*

In the meantime, I took comfort from the story of Jonah. He *also* got swallowed by a fish, but lived to serve God. And what happened to me, back in October of 1986? After being swallowed by a giant tuna — which isn't quite as bad as being eaten alive by a school of codfish (talk with Tom Siddon and John Crosbie on the sellout of the Newfs to the Frenchies) — I became the Comeback Kid! My fish-eating peers elected me the Speaker of the House of Commons!!

True, it took a little time (11 ballots and about 72 hours, if I recall correctly), but they sure wanted me, didn't they? All was forgiven!!

True, my French isn't quite as fluent as John Crosbie's, but so what? I can speak English better than him, any day of the week.

And everyone agrees — at least as of February, 1987, when I am writing this — that I'm doing a bang-up job as Speaker! (Maybe I'd better rephrase that; it was that bearded boy who was banging everybody up, til Brian fed *him* to the sharks, to use another fishy metaphor.) No, let's say that I'm doing a refined, civilized job. Which isn't easy, with the kilograms of flesh which everybody keeps tearing off the federal PCs, nowadays.

Anyway, I'm doing fabulously well. I've served my country as Fisheries Minister — poor Tom's sweating that out now, with the Newfies — and now I'm the very gifted, very unilingual Speaker of the House. And the frills? Why, back in January of this year, I was visited by Mickey Mouse, and made an honorary citizen of Walt Disney World! And after working with stinking fish and Mickey Mouse Members of Parliament every day, I made him feel right at home.

PETER LOUGHEED

What's the tallest mountain in the Rockies? Give up? It's the money mountain known as the Heritage Fund!

It's that kind of outrageous wit which kept me in power for nearly 15 years, until I finally decided to step down from the pinnacle of Western power in 1985. And a pinnacle of power it was, thanks to my amazing ingenuity, intelligence, good looks, wealth, and, most important to success in politics, my old football cronies.

I was born in Calgary in 1928, but, like some others, my roots go back a lot further. In my case a lot deeper as well. My grandfather was Sir James Alexander Lougheed, who had gone west from Ontario a century ago to make over a million smackers in the first land-boom in Calgary. He eventually became a lawyer for the Canadian Pacific Railway, established Alberta's most prestigious corporate law firm, served as a federal senator and Cabinet minister, and became the only Albertan ever to be knighted. He managed to do all this without ever having to throw a football. Hard to believe.

But all great things must come to an end. Our family suffered terrible reverses during the Great Depression, and the old man's 26-room mansion had to be sold off. I lay on the ground weeping, maybe 10 or 11 years old at the time, and vowed that this would never again happen to my family. "Tomorrow," I cried. "Tomorrow at Beaulieu. After all, tomorrow is another day."

And so it was. My father Edgar was also a lawyer but he never made the kind of big bucks that his father had made. But after the Second World War there was an oil boom in Alberta, and Lougheeds began to flourish financially again. By the time my dad passed away, in 1951, his estate was worth over $3 million. Today in Alberta, this would be considered petty cash to most lawyers.

But it was my mom, not dad, who filled me with goals and objectives. Well, maybe *field* goals, and touchdowns. Her name was Edna, and she took great pride in my magnificent athletic career: baseball, track and field, basketball, hockey, and, of course, football. Oh God, but I was good! Many have attributed my passion for winning to my family's always-changing financial situation, and they could be right. But I loved the competition — always did — which is why I went into provincial politics. Federal would have been too easy; the other guys wouldn't have stood a chance.

At the University of Alberta, I was tops in everything: I was president of my fraternity as well as the student council. I got my B.A. degree in 1950, from U. of A., then my LL.B. in 1952, and then got an M.B.A. at Harvard two years later. It was the perfect background for the Man Who Would Save The West.

I articled and then practiced in the mid-50s with a major Calgary law firm, knocking off a few years as a punt returned for the Edmonton Eskimos. Ya gotta stay in shape, ya know. Then I joined the Mannix Corporation in 1956, working my way up from junior counsel to general counsel to VP to director by 1960. *Another touchdown by Peter Lougheed of the Eskies!!!*

By 1962, I'd had enough of working in a place where someone else's name was on the masthead. I joined the law firm of Moore, Lougheed, Atkinson & Tingle. And that's where it began — then I started to get the political itch.

You see, the Progressive Conservative Party of Alberta had been near-death ever since the Social Credit party took power some three decades earlier. I was attracted to the party since my grandfather had some Tory connections, and, to be honest with you, I've always enjoyed taking something limp and lifeless in hand and bringing it to life. I did it for the Eskimos, I did it for the provincial party, but I have to admit that I failed to do it for Joe Clark. Well, that's the way life goes, as the French say.

After organizing dozens of meetings to plan all aspects of revivifying the party, I took over the leadership of the provincial PC organization in March of 1965, and began one of the greatest comebacks since Lazarus. Of course, Lazarus had only Jesus behind *him*; the Alberta Tories had a Lougheed.

It would take six more years to get my government elected, but look how long it took Richard Nixon to make a comeback, after losing to Kennedy. I'm not too pleased with that comparison.

The Calgary *Herald* called it "Alberta's longest election campaign," and it sure seemed like that. Our first opening was in the May 1967 provincial election, when I ran successfully in the riding of Calgary West and entered the Alberta legislature with five other colleagues. Not a full football team, yet. If I had been into basketball, we'd have had a team already.

Like all good politicians, I learned all my lessons from the New Democratic Party, who had never done very well in Alberta, but who really knew how to cover the streets and solicit every door for support. (The Alberta Tories used to *lean* against *one* door for support, which never translated into very many votes.)

It's true, the Socreds still controlled 55 of the 65 seats in the provincial legislature, but we had managed to increase our share of the vote from 13% back in 1963, when we hadn't won a single seat, up to 26.3%. Why, we even replaced the Grits as the official opposition, may their Western souls rest in pieces.

By 1971, my Tories were ready to take on the provincial Socreds, who were by then being led by Harry Strom. We had a platform as complex as a federal income tax form: We would make the government more responsive. We would give more powers to the cities. We would bring Albertans fully into the mainstream of Canadian life. We would put gas into every garage, and oil into every pot. The cars and chickens would have to come later.

This was the beginning of my love affair with television. I took lessons on how to look natural in front of the camera, how to read the cue cards smoothly, how to eat natural crunchy granola before going on the air. We spent 85% of our advertising budget on television, and it began to pay off. By early summer, 1971, polls showed that I was the third most recognizable figure on Alberta television, just after Lorne Greene and Road Runner. And two of us were Canadian!

On August 30, 1971, the extraordinary upset took place: My Tories took 49 of the 75 seats in the recently enlarged legislature. The Socreds were down to 25, the NDP was down to one, and the Grits were gone with the wind. It would take a bit longer to get the bastards out of Ottawa. But thirty-six years of Social Credit rule was over; my thousand year reich had begun!

My victory captured the changing mood of the province; we were moving from a rural society to an urban one, and from the farm to the oil field. Both can stink up your shoes, however. I promptly reached out and brought in the best men available, from all the best backgrounds: High school chums. Former football teammates. Buddies from Mannix. People who had had the common sense and intelligence to work and play with me over the previous two decades. And, by God, we would now work and play together for Alberta.

We Albertans were sick and tired of being pushed around by the non-oil-producing fairies of the East. We had *had* it with Quebec, Ontario, the Feds. We had to have greater autonomy within Confederation, or the Easterners better start thinking about building pipelines from Saudi Arabia.

We also passed a new Bill of Rights, to protect the rights of individuals *even if they had voted Socred in the past.* (Had to fight hard to get that latter bit in; a lot of us Tories never forget.) We passed laws to beef up the agricultural sector and to control the environment. But most important, we had to shift the Albertan economy away from its heavy dependence on oil and gas, and yet make energy more profitable at the same time. This was known in Biblical times as threading a camel through the eye of a needle.

Then a wonderful thing happened. Or at least we in Alberta thought it was wonderful. The Oil Producing and Exporting Countries (I love you, a barrel and OPEC!) suddenly created an oil crisis in 1973. There were long lines at gas stations across North America, and people cursed and raged. But not us Albertans! No, sir, we thought the oil shortage was beautiful! It just goes to show how forgiving we can be toward our beloved Arab brothers, may Allah be praised.

We had been bowing and scraping to the East, for the past few decades; let those fairies east of Kenora go humble for a while and see what it felt like! We were finally able to use our energy supplies as a lever to force a readjustment in our economic relationship with Eastern Canada. Or did we use oil and gas as a lever to beat them with? I forget.

But we had other worries: Some forecasters saw that our sources would last for only another decade or two. By Allah, we wanted the world market price for our gas and oil. We wanted to save for the future and the hereafter. (We Canadians have always been great savers; look at the football memorabilia in my office.)

Now, the BNA Act of 1867 promised that each province should have control over its own natural resources but the idiots in Ottawa kept trying to fake to the left.

Then, on September 13, 1973, the limp-wristed Grits in Ottawa imposed a 40¢ per barrel tax on our oil that was being exported to the U.S., with the proceeds going to mitigate the effects of rising energy prices in the *Eastern* provinces! It was a day that would live in infamy! (Like that line!) I was enraged, and called the move the most discriminatory action taken by the Feds against any one province in the history of Confederation. Actually, what they did to Louis Riel wasn't very nice, either.

Then, in the fall of the following year, the feather-brained Feds actually decided to phase out oil experts to the States! Jeez! And just a few weeks after that, the Ottawa No-nothings disallowed the deduction of provincial royalties from taxable corporate income! What could I do? So I reduced my province's levies on the oil producers, so they wouldn't jump from very high windows. I considered challenging Ottawa the way it deserved, but I couldn't find any modern-day Guy Fawkes to treat our federal Parliament the way it so richly deserved.

But Ottawa soon got a message from us. In the 1974 election, when my fellow Canadians sent Pierre Elliott Disaster back with a majority, Alberta returned 19 Tories and not a single Grit to Parliament. Allah Be Praised! And in the provincial election of March, 1975, my Conservatives took 69 of the 75 seats. And we didn't need Ferdinand Marcos to handle the vote-counting, either.

Right after that election, I decided that if you can't beat 'em in the alleys of Ottawa, beat 'em in Europe. So I took 55 true Albertans across the pond, and we wowed the natives with our mastery of energy and political matters. Even Ottawa learned something. In 1976, they finally agreed to permit domestic oil and gas prices to rise gradually to world market levels. This stimulated productivity in Alberta — More Bucks. But it was like drilling through bedrock to get those idiots to agree to anything. Thank God at least I had the Edmonton *Journal* in my right pocket, and Teddy Byfield and his *Alberta Report* in my *back* pocket. (There *are* no left pockets in this province.)

But I couldn't sit around and wait for the feds. No, I went ahead with a number of extraordinary actions. For one, I bought Pacific Western Airlines at a bargain sale. This guaranteed that the men and women of Alberta could move about. The free passes from Air Canada and CP Air to Hawaii back in 1978 were clearly a necessity, as you can see; PWA just didn't fly that far. Yet.

I also invested over $1 billion in Syncrude, which was a super idea to exploit oil sands along the Athabaska River. I'm out of power now, so I never *did* find out whatever happened to that project. It seemed like a great idea at the time.

My other big move was to fulfill my campaign promise back in the 1975 election: to set up an Alberta Heritage Savings Trust Fund. I instituted it in 1976, financed with 30% of the government's annual energy revenues. I soon had more billions than I knew what to do with. But I had lots of old cronies to take care of the money — and when you're talking billions, you're talking *real* money — and they invested it well, often at rates as high as the rate of inflation. Or at least nearly as high.

There have been the occasional unfair swipes at my inspired leadership — but never by Alberta papers, of course — and they can all be easily explained away. I personally see nothing wrong with accepting lifts aboard the Nova executive jet, since they were going that way, anyway. And the fact that my government purchased my grandfather's mansion as a historic site for quite a bit more than its assessed value just proves what a good business mind I have. And besides, why would I need the money? I got all I needed to live on, by suing the C.B.C. over that 1977 slander, *Tarsands*.

It's true, the occasional MLA in my government would say nasty things about French Canadians, or about native people, but, to be fair, being in public office does not mean that you have to check your feelings and mouth at the door.

Prince Peter, they called me. The King. but I was merely the leader of the Alberta Progressive Conservative Party, that's all, and I refused to let it go to my head. Although, to be frank about it, it is an awesome responsibility to have the power of life and death over the most important province in Canada. The fact that Canada was not the most important *country on earth* is partly my fault, I'm willing to admit; I had the chance to run for my party's federal leadership, and foolishly chose not to. And Joe Clark foolishly *did*.

I've also been accused, falsely, of course, of being tinged with separatism. Nothing could be further from the truth. I was and still am very pro-Canadian, just so long as each Canadian can afford at least 50¢ a litre for gas. Make that 75¢ a litre.

I've even been slurred as "Pinko Pete," due to my heavy involvement with the economy. But that is absurd, of course. It's my duty
to keep down expenditures on education and day care. It's my duty
to deny government employees the right to strike. If I'm pink, then
Joe Clark and Brian Mulroney are so red, they can visit the Soviet
Union without a visa.

The Alberta voters sure didn't buy any of those slurs; in the
March, 1979 election, my party took 74 out of the 79 provincial
seats, and in the November, 1982 election, I won 75 out of 79. I
had hoped to win every single seat before I finally retired, but one
must accept one's lot. And 75 seats is a lot.

Do you think the public fully understood just how difficult it was,
to be Premier of this country's most important province? Consider
my astonishing itinerary in 1983, alone: I had to take a lengthy trip
to Hawaii. Then it was off to New York City, London, Zurich and
Geneva. That cost $100,000 in public funds, including over $1400
for my wife Jeanne, who just *hates* when I travel alone. Then I had
to spend five long weeks in China, Japan and Hong Kong that summer at a cost of nearly a quarter of a million dollars, since I had
to take so many old football players with me. (But no reporters;
they only cause trouble and bad PR.) And I then had to go to New
York again, as well as Washington and California. It was hectic being
Premier of Alberta, but maybe it was all for the best. There was
all this nonsense over John Faulkner, Neil Crawford and George
de Rappard, and I would have only been embarrassed, had I stayed
in town.

Anyway, I've handed the reigns of Absolute Power to my good
friend and former Edmonton Eskimo teammate Don Getty, so I
know that Right will continue to Prevail. There is an Alberta town
named Lougheed and a mountain named Lougheed, and even
though the Lougheed they were named after was my granddad, it's
still nice to know that my name will live on in this province.

So now it's directorships for big hitting companies across the country. I can't complain. I get to sit in on meetings once every few
months for an afternoon and collect $10,000 to $20,000 a throw.
It's a living.

Sure I miss the shoulder-patting, the fist-jabbing, and, most of
all, the ass-patting, of politics. Or was that football? Anyways, there

is a Conservative government in Ottawa and a Conservative government — now and forever — in Alberta, and all's right with the world. Not far right, mind you, but right. And right, as every Alberta Tory knows, at the drop of an oil barrel, makes might.

I've passed the ball to you, Don. Run for it. And remember our old adage: "When in doubt, punt."

Well, it worked with the Eskies.

Straight from Down Under

ED SCHREYER

I SHALL RETURN!

Straight from the Fast Shuffle

ERIK NIELSEN

For nearly three decades, I have been the Scourge of Parliament, making Grits shiver in their mukluks. I'm now the third-longest-serving Member of Parliament, and if I had my way, I'd still be around, long after the Evil Legacy of Pierre Elliott Communist is a forgotten memory. Of course, I've spent most of my life in the hell of Opposition, so it wasn't easy for me to learn to cope with the Heaven of Governing. But I sure tried.

My father came from Denmark, which is even further North than Canada. My grandfather had been a shoemaker, and my father rebelled, by becoming an acrobat in a circus. I myself rebelled, by combining the best of both jobs: I nail my opponents to the floor, and I juggle half a dozen Parliamentary duties at any one time. That's a joke, son.

My father came to this grand country around the time of the First World War, and joined the Royal North West Mounted Police, now called the RCMP. I've had a lifelong interest in that great institution. He began with the rank of "boy," and had the job of cleaning out the crap from the horses' stables. This led to my lifelong interest in the great career of Joe Clark.

He married a Welsh woman — my future mother — and she quickly had three sons, before Constable Nielsen was transferred up to Fort Norman, about 200 miles below the Arctic Circle, on the Mackenzie River. He must have done something that really pissed off his boss; it was colder than hell up there.

We spoke English at home and Dogrib in the settlement, which is about the most useless second language for political success that I can think of. Some years later, after we half-froze to death a few hundred times, my father was transferred to Edmonton, and eventually we all lived on a farm just to the north of the city. It was pretty damned cold down there, as well.

My dad remained a Mountie for 30 years, and eventually retired, and operated a small detective agency in Edmonton. It was a great help; I loved to use him to get the goods on Trudeau and his henchmen.

All three of us Nielsen boys joined the Royal Canadian Air Force, and I had decided to make the Air Force my career, but they kept advancing junior officers over me. I guess I tended to rub everyone the wrong way even before I entered Parliament. Anyway, I took some law courses at Dalhousie, in the late 40s, and I eventually left the service during the Korean War.

It was 1951; what was I to do? Well, I'd always enjoyed the North, and, to be blunt about it, I had all these old fur coats, snowshoes and galoshes which were just going to waste, sitting out in Halifax. So I wrote letters to various law firms in the West and North, and ended up with the only practicing lawyer in Whitehorse.

By 1957, at the age of 34, I decided to run for Parliament. I didn't think I'd lose, but with the help of hundreds of dead voters who traditionally cast their ballots for the Liberal candidate, I lost by 58 votes. The irregularities — that's Dogrib for Dead Voters — were discovered, and the Speaker declared the seat vacant. I soon won it. And immediately became one of the best-loved Members of Parliament, terrorizing the Opposition, picking fights with the Speaker, beating up little old ladies on Sparks Street. But I really came into my own, when we were back in Opposition, after 1963. It's always more fun to destroy than create, that's what I say.

And I had fun! The Grits tapped our lines, we eavesdropped on their caucus, it was a game really. And it was all so long ago. Anyway, what I did in the sixties isn't important. I was just following orders, that's all. I'm good at that.

And as for my being relieved of my duties in the Cabinet, last June, let's get one thing straight: I wanted to go. I asked to go. I desired to go.

And as of January, 1987, I've decided to throw in the towel, which was pretty well covered with blood, anyway. I wasn't too charmed by the way Brian overruled me on the Sinclair Stevens case, and ordered a judicial inquiry into the affair, and I've had my hands full over the past few months up at Quiet Lake, with my new bride Shelley. (Now you know why I was briefly hospitalized last October with fatigue.)

Anyway, I may have left politics, but the profound influence which I've had on the field has remained, has it not? I mean, just look at the way Mulroney first tried to avoid commenting on why he dumped Bissonette! It kind of paralleled how I so successfully handled the Sinc Stevens affair by pursing my lips together — *just so.*

So that's it. I'm done with politics — forever.

No more Mr. Nice Guy.

DAVID CROMBIE

In the June, 1986 cabinet shuffle, I was moved from Indians to Japanese. Let me explain: My new post is Secretary of State with responsibilities for multiculturalism. This means that I have the joy of trying to figure out how to redress the Japanese-Canadians who were wrongly interned during the Second World War.

I can't stand it! My ass is going to fry, because of something we did four decades ago, during the war!

I need some expert advice on this, and I need it *fast*.

I'm calling Kurt Waldheim.

JOE CLARK

Can you imagine what it's like to peak at 39? Sure, Jack Benny did that, but at least *he* managed to stay there for another four decades. True, a lot of hockey and baseball players peak at 25 or 30, but that's different; that's sports. But this — no matter *what* Peter Lougheed and Don Getty might tell you — is *not* sports — it's politics. And politics is my life. Which is part of the problem. Actually, it's most of it.

You see, politics is what I have lived and breathed, almost since the day I was born, in June, 1939. It was an eventful year in international affairs, with World War II looming on the horizon, and it would be an eventful year in the future of Canadian politics, with my birth. Or so I had hoped. Dammit.

My birthplace was High River, Alberta, a community of communities, about 30 miles south of Calgary. My grandfather on my dad's side, Charles Clark, was of Scottish origin — and *they* never could get along with the Irish, either. (Just joking, Brian.) He had moved from Kincardine, Ontario, west to High River, to operate a horse ranch. (Even then, we Clarks were knee deep in it.) He didn't make any money from that, so he began a weekly newspaper, the High River *Times*, in 1905. In his second job, he did well; I seem to be having better luck in my second job, too: External Affairs. So far, so good.

My parents were Charles A. and Grace R. Clark, and they had one other child, my younger brother Peter, who, alas, didn't turn out too well at all: He's a Calgary lawyer. (Another joke, Pete.) My mom says that I was "an ordinary kid," which is the kind of press I could have done without, back when I was Prime Minister of this Great Land, back in the late '70s and early '80s. (You can see just how generous I can be, when I want to.)

I learned politics at my mother's knee. It was then that I decided that I wanted to knee the Grits and Socialists. Mum would pass the sugar and whisper to me, "Sugar is like the Liberals: It seems sweet, but it can kill you." I loved to go camping, even though I was never very athletic. Except for my feet, which I've since managed to solve, with some medical assistance. When other kids my age would talk about becoming policemen or firemen, I used to talk about being Prime Minister. Which, as Mordecai Richler once stated, was "limiting one's options rather greatly at a young age." But I didn't care; I wanted to be Prime Minister before I turned 40, and *I made it!* The fact that I was an ex-Prime Minister before I turned 41 has been less of a pleasure. More on that later. *Don't rush me.*

I had politics in my blood, and even penicillin didn't help. My dad had worked for the Progressive Conservatives, and a great uncle had served for a decade as the MP for Bruce County, Ontario. So how could I lose when I had such a good quotient of brains? (I recently heard from a cousin that I was reading when I was 3½. If only I knew how to *count* — like that time after Crosbie presented our budget and we needed the votes in the House.)

When I was only 16, while other kids were busy getting pimples, I was busy giving speeches. My first public talk won me a trip to Ottawa, sponsored by the Rotary Club. While I was there, I met such luminaries as John Diefenbaker — another great politician whose party treated him shabbily. While I was in that exciting city (look, I'm from High River, not Guelph; to me, even *Ottawa* looked good), I watched a key parliamentary debate in which the Liberals crushed the Tory opposition. I vowed to avenge this insult on our country's manhood. Right, Maureen?

I returned home and cried to my mother, "We don't *have* democracy in this country. It's run by one party, and it should have an effective and strong opposition!" Just my luck; for most of my adult life, Canada has *continued* to have one party running it, and I've been primarily stuck in opposition.

The die was cast. The Rubicon, or at least High River, had been crossed. In 1957, soon after I entered the University of Alberta in Edmonton, I became active in the Tory club on campus. There I was, standing on the quadrangle, handing out Diefenbaker pamphlets for hours and hours to anyone who would take one. God, it was a great way to meet girls!! Oh, sorry, Maureen. It was a great way to meet *women*. (God, but these girls can be tough to satisfy.)

In the summer of 1956, I had worked for the Calgary *Herald*, and in other summers for the Edmonton *Journal* and for the Canadian

Press Bureau in Calgary. No one ever confiscated anything over there. My big thrill was in 1959, when I served as the chauffeur of W.J.C. Kirby, the PC leader in Alberta, gaining valuable political experience. I was in the driver's seat, at last!

I graduated with a B.A. in history in 1960, but found that I had to attend the University of Alberta for an extra year to get my grades up high enough for graduate school. It was either that, or I'd be able to do nothing better in my life than politics. In the fall of 1961, after I was denied admission to Georgetown University in Washington, D.C. — they'll be sorry they did that; I'll get them back, now that I'm in External Affairs — I went off to Europe. It wasn't much of a Grand Tour, though; I wrapped packages at Harrod's in London, studied English in England and French in France. I learned how to wrap packages really well.

Returning to Canada in early 1962, I worked at the Progressive Conservative headquarters in Ottawa, writing campaign literature in the 1962 general election, and trying to get on the good side of Dalton Camp. That fall, I entered Dalhousie Law School in Halifax, but found it neither interesting nor challenging. They didn't like me too much, either. You see, I was doing so much travel on behalf of the Tories, I didn't attend classes regularly, so I flunked Dal's attendance requirements. Well, at least I didn't ruin our country's economy, like Pierre Trudeau. Which is *worse*, I ask you?

I still managed to serve as president of the Progressive Conservative Student Federation from 1962 to 1965, and was the founding chairman of the Canadian Political Youth Council in 1964. That same year, I was secretary of the National Conference on Canadian Goals in Fredericton. Who needed university degrees? And besides, the Tories didn't insist on high grades. They never have, either, as you can readily see. Look at guys like Bill Domm, for instance.

From 1965 to 1967, I taught political science at the University of Alberta, and started getting deeply involved in my province's politics. We just *had* to break the hold of the Social Credit party, which had run the province since 1935! What did they think they were, the Progressive Conservatives of Ontario? (Of blessed memory.) I was directly responsible for Peter Lougheed making it to the premiership soon after. And what thanks did I get? Don't ask.

I worked 18 hours a day, organizing constituencies and policies. We decided to go door to door, making it clear that we were a good alternative to the Social Credits, instead of just attacking them. It was all my idea, and I'd like to thank here the NDP for giving it to me.

I not only campaigned for my good friend Peter — or so I thought he was — but I, myself, entered the race for the Alberta Provincial Assembly. The seat was then occupied by the Assembly Speaker, Art Dixon, of the ruling Socreds. And as every student of physics will tell you, two bodies cannot occupy the same space. Darn it.

I took the difficulty in stride, however, with my customary good humour and rapier wit. When I asked a pollster if I had a chance of winning, he told me, "Well, there was, after all, a virgin birth." Actually, the humour and wit was that of the pollster, wasn't it?

But I ran as though I *did* have a chance: I knocked on over 10,000 doors in the month and a half of campaigning, and quite a number of the voters were home. Most were not. I lost by a mere 461 votes, which was really quite amazing. But not amazing enough. I *had* hoped to change the name of the riding to Bethlehem.

Lougheed won *his* race, though, by a huge margin, and the Progressive Conservatives became the official opposition of Alberta, with a walloping half-dozen seats out of the total of 65.

During that same year, I also served as a special assistant to Davie Fulton, a famous drinker at the pool of Canadian politics. He had been Minister of Justice and Attorney General in Ottawa, and was running for the leadership of the Progressive Conservatives. And he did almost as well as I did, back in the Alberta race. I was troubled by the campaign to push out John Diefenbaker — how was I to know that history would repeat itself with me? — and I responded in the best way I knew how: I half-heartedly supported it.

Thank heavens, the eventual replacement, Robert Stanfield, was really impressed with my political acumen. (It wasn't *easy* to half-heartedly support the knifing of someone; maybe it should have entered Dief's back only three or four centimetres?) Bob liked me so much, he not only gave me a life supply of underwear and long-johns, but he hired me as his executive assistant and speech writer. I immediately earned his appreciation by recommending that he add bananas to his daily diet, and I used to toss footballs to him all the time, to keep him in shape. Here it is, nearly two decades later, and the political cartoonists of Canada continue to send me thank-you notes for doing it.

I worked in Ottawa for the next three years in that position, which was a thrilling time for me: I got to put my own words — and bananas — in the mouth of the Opposition Leader of the federal Progressive Conservative Party! Then, in 1970, I left the nation's capital once more and toured Europe, still trying to conquer French. I'm not sure why I had so much trouble; the Nazis did it in just a few days. But I *had* to learn that language; I *had* to! How else would I ever be able to talk with Jean Chrétien? I couldn't understand *a word* he said in English, and it seemed like he was worth listening to.

In late 1970, I finished off my M.A. degree in political science at the University of Alberta, and I made the Big Decision: There were no jobs for university teachers anywhere; it would have to be the political arena. I decided to seek a PC nomination for the federal House of Commons. I chose the riding of Rocky Mountain because it was so close to my family home of High River, and also because the riding had been Conservative since before Confederation. Since before the white man came, in fact. Or so I had thought at the time.

I used an inspired strategy: I had the nomination proceedings take place in nearly a dozen meetings all across the huge riding, so no other candidate could pack any single meeting. And it worked! Now, all I had to do was beat the Liberal incumbent, Allen Sulatychy. (Yes, there actually *were* elected Grits in Alberta back then.)

Fortunately for me, no one could spell his name. On October 30, 1972, I defeated him by over 5,000 votes. I had won! I finally had a job! A real job! Well, okay; a *paying* job.

I made an immediate impact on Ottawa, and soon became known as "A Man as Exciting as His Name." I was named chairman of the Conservative caucus committee on youth in early 1973 — I looked so youthful! And in July, 1974, I was re-elected to my parliamentary seat, leading to my appointment as chairman of the PC caucus committee on the environment. Wow! I was making *waves*. Right, Maureen? And I was getting well known around Parliament Hill.

And speaking of Maureen — my beloved wife — I married Ms

McTeer, and almost changed her name to mine, in 1973. She is beautiful, bright and youthful, and she can type, too. (That's only a joke, Maureen.) She is a great asset to me, and is probably the main reason why I'm often called "the man behind the woman."

By 1975, I decided that I had waited long enough: nearly three years. So I made my biggest move, and declared my candidacy for the leadership of the federal PCs. My announcement made the comic page in the Ottawa *Journal* and the women's section of the High River *Times*. The last one really *hurt*. To be fair to me, the paper had been sold, back in 1966, so my family no longer ran it.

No one thought I had a chance. Indeed, Jimmy the Greek didn't even name any odds on my campaign. There were a dozen, in all, reaching mightily for the reigns of powerlessness, now that Bob Stanfield had decided to step down. Claude Wagner had the largest following, not to mention a far better French accent that I, but he was a bit right-wing. In fact, some of my colleagues believe that *Ed Broadbent* is a bit right-wing, when compared with me.

But the delegates wanted what I had: Middle-class values. A man of the centre. Personal integrity. (To tell the truth, a lot of guys voted for me because they thought that it was terrific for a man to be living with a woman who had a different last name. They thought it was sexy and indiscreet, and the Progressive Conservatives needed both those qualities.)

I fought for what the people wanted: A decrease in government spending. Fewer economic controls. Limits on the right of public employees to go on strike. I also fought for what lots of delegates did not want: I supported the *Official Languages Act*. Reform of Canada's anti-abortion laws. (What I don't do for you, Maureen!) Rejection of capital punishment. (Quite a few delegates wanted to kill me for that. *You* figure it out.)

On the first ballot, the field was narrowed to just five candidates, with Wagner still leading. But that trust fund set up for him began to hurt Claude, and it got me wondering: Why hadn't anyone ever done that for *me*? By the fourth ballot, I had clobbered Wagner by a vote of 1187 to 1122, a mighty mandate of 65 votes. And most important: I had Dalton Camp on my side. You just can't *imagine* how important that is in my party.

113

My first priority was to pull together the caucus, which with the Progressive Conservatives, is just as easy as getting Maureen to change her name to mine. I decided to spend less time in Parliament — where the rotten Grits were in power, anyway — and more time, travelling across this great country of Canada, getting my face in the papers and taking the first extended vacation I had had in years.

A lot of people in my party complained that I should have stayed in Ottawa and fought the Liberals, but they were managing to do that all by themselves, with cabinet ministers asking federal judges for various favours, and lots more. I wanted to take the high road. Or the High River road, if you will.

I wanted to do it *my* way, as that great Canadian, Frank Sinatra, once wrote. In June of 1976, I visited President Gerald Ford and his boss, Henry Kissinger, and they both responded the same way to me and our meeting. They wanted to know who I was.

Maureen and I made ourselves at home at Stornaway and lived there happily until the 1979 election, when we happily gave it up for 22 Sussex Avenue. Then we were suddenly in Stornaway again, and it was as if we had never left.

Which leads me to my time as Prime Minister, which I would just as soon not discuss, but I'm afraid that I have to. By 1979, the Liberals had crumbled in popularity, and it was clearly time for a change. Indeed, oil and lube jobs went up 45% during the election campaign.

I had become known as *"The Man Inarticulate in Both Official Languages,"* and men and women right across Canada knew that I was about to replace Pierre Trudeau in power. True, it wasn't a smashing victory, but we *did* win a handsome minority, you've got to admit! I still remember what I told the cheering crowds that wonderful evening: That we would function as if we had a majority. What a great idea *that* was. Right, Maureen?

The following months, as I served as the Prime Minister of Canada, I did a number of memorable things. For example, I fearlessly decided to move the Canadian Embassy in Israel from Tel Aviv to Jerusalem. (Although Bob Stanfield ultimately urged me not to, it seemed like a smart move. After all, Jerusalem *is* the capital of Israel. And we *had* to defeat John Roberts in his Forest

Hill riding. And anyway, who do these Arabs think they are, threatening to boycott Canada? We decided not to.)

What else? Oh, yes. I made a number of decisions about what to do with Petro-Canada, a lot of them rather contradictory. But I still made those crisp decisions.

I had a number of heavy discussions with Alberta and Ontario over energy questions, which didn't seem to satisfy the football player very much. But that's the way we Tories are!

Then there was our tough budget, which never managed to be put into practice, due to a misinformed vote in Parliament. Never did trust the Creditistes.

Anyway, it seems clear that my most positive act as Prime Minister was my not calling Parliament back into session during the first six months after the election.

But let's be fair. *Please.* I *did* get the Americans out of the Canadian embassy in Teheran, remember. And how about my boycott of the 1980 Olympic Games in Moscow? That sure got those Russkies out of Afghanistan, didn't it?

Moreover, Trudeau had just quit; who would have guessed that the bad penny would return?

Okay, so I *did* lose the 1980 election. But a lot of Tories *did* win re-election in their ridings, including myself. Even though I won in Yellowhead, and not in Bow River, due to that silly feud with Stan Schumacher, back in 1976. And didn't Quebec give us *one whole seat*, and *over 12% of the vote*?

By 1980, I was the Leader of the Official Opposition again, which is still a pretty good job, with lots of perks. I was now known as *"the man who got our boys out of Teheran and our Tories out of power."* I argued brilliantly that I had learned from our mistakes, and the party seemed to agree that I had learned an astounding amount.

But I had had *enough* of being humiliated by the Grits; my fellow Tories would soon demand their turn. In 1981, there was a leadership vote, and I received the resounding support of over 66% of my fellow Progressive Conservatives. It was an amazing victory — it should only have happened against Trudeau! — but no, it wasn't good enough. I fought from coast to coast over the next two years, and by 1983, my leadership support was up to over 66%.

I decided not to stand pat; I wanted 100% backing, or nothing.

115

So I called for a Leadership Convention in June of 1983, determined to win the praise of everyone in my party, or die trying. And I've always felt that being in your early 40s is a bit young to die.

Sure, I could have clung to power; look at how much Canadians love cling peaches. But I had no choice: I wanted to show my strength by forcing my opponents into the open, and defeating them, in order to unify the party. Maybe even Maureen would change her name to mine at last. There were sure a lot of men and women in the Tory party who wanted to change their leader's name *from* mine.

There were difficult moments. Like when I was booed for speaking in French at Massey Hall in Toronto. Or was it just because I was speaking at all? I can't recall.

I still remember the cries of my supporters: "Give me a J! Give me an O! Give me an E!. Whaddayagot??" A lot of them weren't quite sure at the time and kept yelling "Brian."

The convention didn't turn out as I had hoped. Everyone seemed to gang up on me, and I now understood how Dief must have felt. Gamble moved to Mulroney's camp, and then Pocklington and then Crombie — he never really did forgive me for not giving him a bigger cabinet post, did he? — moved to Crosbie before moving to Mulroney. Hell, Crosbie couldn't even speak French! To tell the truth, I've never had much success with that language, either.

In the fourth ballot, Mulroney won. Maureen and I were out of Stornoway once more, except this time, it wasn't 22 Sussex that I was moving into. Ottawa real estate can get rather confusing after a while.

But what did Brian Mulroney have that I didn't have? OK, so he's slick. So he's exciting. So he's good-looking. So his wife stays at home and changed her name. (Right, Maureen?)

But that's all blood over the damn, as they say. Brian, at least, had sense enough to make me External Affairs Minister, and the world is now my oyster. So from Prime Minister to Cabinet Minister isn't all that bad. I still get to be called "The Right Honourable Joseph Clark." And I was P.M. longer than John Turner, *so there!!* And didn't I make the cover of *Maclean's* in late 1986? And they even said I was doing a good job!!

Politics is pretty chancy in this country, especially if you're a Progressive Conservative. But it's what I've always said: "I'm like that warm wind that pushes back the cold wind in Alberta. It's called a chinook. And that's what *I* am; a chinook."

I just wish that people would stop pronouncing it in one syllable.

JOHN TURNER

Sure I've made some mistakes in my 57 years. Not becoming a priest, for one. Saving John Diefenbaker from drowning during that Caribbean holiday, for another. Losing the 1968 Liberal leadership race was a third. Not ever having the chance to watch Pierre Trudeau drown. And calling a federal election in the summer of 1984.

But didn't Mike Pearson say that I would someday be Prime Minister? And was he not right? Of course, he didn't say how long I would be Prime Minister, which is something that I will always have to live with. As is Geills, who makes it all worthwhile. Almost.

Which leads me to the Big Questions. How could the man voted The Most Popular Student at the University of British Columbia in 1948, be so crushed in a popular vote, on September the 4th, 1984? How could a man who did such wonders in the Justice Department to extend rights to individuals, keep his mouth shut when the War Measures Act was pushed through by Trudeau? How could a man with such gorgeous blue eyes and silvery hair and solid chin be Prime Minister for less time than Joe Clark, who lacks all three? If you expect me to answer these questions in a self-serving autobiographical sketch, you are probably crazy enough to think that Pierre and I are best friends.

No, what you are going to get here is the remarkable history of the 17th Prime Minister of Canada, the Right Honourable John Napier Turner. If you want to read even more, may I recommend *John Turner, The Long Run*, by that fine journalist Jack Cahill (McClelland & Stewart, 234 pages, $19.95), remaindered for around 99¢ at a bookstore near you. Just think: a $20 hardcover book, with lots of great photos, for less than a buck. And they accused me of causing runaway inflation, back in the 70s, when I was Finance Minister! What a joke! A-he-he-he-he-he. A-he-he-he-he-he.

Sorry; I'm trying to stop that nervous laugh. But the idea that Jean Chrétien could have a best-seller, when he didn't even win the leadership of the party, and that book about me nearly ruined Jack McClelland, just underlines the sort of injustices I had to fight, when

I set up the National Law Reform Commission, back in 1970 or so. But even a man like me doesn't have all the answers. Most. But not all.

Most people know of my birth in Surrey, England, in June of 1929, to the brilliant and beautiful Phyllis Gregory Turner. She returned to Canada with me after my father died and joined the Tariff Board in Ottawa, later administrating oils and fats on the War Prices and Trade Board under Mackenzie King, in the 1940s. Just think of it! A gifted economist, being forced to handle oils and fats! I vowed then to avenge this injustice in my own career, by oiling my way into high political life, and by hanging around with the fat cats on Bay Street.

I grew up steeped in politics, primarily Liberal. Although R.B. Bennett ran after mom for a while, in the hopes of getting her to marry him. Boy, that sure would have ruined my political future, even before it began. A-he-he-he-he. A-he-he-he-he. (Sorry.)

C.D. Howe used to hang around our house, tossing difficult mathematical questions at me, such as "What's a million?" We would summer up in the Gatineau Hills in a rented cottage, right next door to Lester Pearson's. And as a young lad — handsome and athletic, even back then — I used to walk my dog, often running into William Lyon Mackenzie King walking his. Actually, he was *talking* to his, as I remember.

Contrary to some of the Tory slurs against me, we didn't have very much money back then. But my mom still managed to send me to the most prestigious private schools in our nation's capital. By the time I was 16, I was off to the University of British Columbia, the only province that was as beautiful as I was. Another reason was that my mom had married an industrialist from that province, and the family had moved there.

I played ice hockey. I won national championships for running the 100 and 200 yard dashes. I wrote sports articles. I was fought over by fraternities. I won a Rhodes scholarship in 1949. I patted all the girls on their fannies, and they just loved it. Honestly. A-he-he-he-he-he. (Sorry.)

They called me "Chick" Turner, and I was adored by everyone who knew me, and even by those who didn't. As someone wrote in the *Ubyssey*, the university newspaper, "He rolls sportsmanship, scholarship and leadership into a handsome package that has made him undoubtedly the university's most popular student." Is there any wonder why I'm fond of journalists?

I did everything right: I got a BA in jurisprudence from Oxford; toured Europe as a member of an Oxford-Cambridge track team; studied French civil law at the Sorbonne. Why they didn't elect me as Prime Minister of Canada back then, I have no idea.

But Canadians are slow to recognize excellence, as was seen in my later loss of the leadership race in 1968. There was one major incident, before that date. I danced with Princess Margaret at my step-father's ball, in 1958, and helped launch her career. She was a so-so dancer, and probably would have done better if she had married me, but that's the way it goes.

I won my first race for Parliament in 1962, in the Montreal riding of St. Lawrence-St. George, and married one of the volunteers in my campaign the following year. Geills has been volunteering to work for me ever since, and although I can't blame her, I can't thank her enough, either. Thanks, Geills.

Within three years, I was in Mike Pearson's cabinet; within another three years, I was running for my party's leadership. I got 195 votes, which wasn't very much, but I improved on it somewhat, by 1984. Pierre Trudeau won that leadership race, as I recall. A-he-he-he-he-he-he-he. (Sorry.)

My list of successes in my various ministries could fill a book, and they have, too. (See the Cahill reference, above.) I was superb as Registrar General in 1967; magnificent as Minister of Consumer and Corporate Affairs in 1968; wonderful as Minister of Justice from 1968 to 1972; inspired as Minister of Finance from 1972 to 1975, and fantastic as a corporate lawyer in Toronto, from 1975 to 1984.

What happened between Pierre and myself at that private meeting on September 10, 1975, has been a source of considerable speculation and curiosity, over the years. But I am not about to bad-mouth a man who led this country so ably down the garden path. No, the bastard simply refused to go along with my call for stringent controls on inflation, and a cutting down of his insanely excessive government spending. I had expected the sonovabitch to refuse to accept my offer to resign, and be assured of more support in my monumental struggle against inflation. But the turd actually accepted my resignation, and insulted me with an offer of a judgeship or a Senate seat. No, I won't bad-mouth the incompetent buffoon, or mention the fact that just a few months later, the numbskull announced a policy of strict wage and price controls, proving me right.

I was the Prince in Exile over the next decade, with tens of millions across Canada waiting breathlessly for me to emerge from the 38th floor at McMillan, Binch, where I was making tens of millions. Occasionally I alienated a good friend with my criticisms, such as that time when I attacked the destructive policies of Jean Chrétien, but he knew that I was only kidding, and so did I. Jean and I remain good friends to this day, don't we? Don't we? What do you have to say, Jean? A-he-he-he-he-he-he-he. (Sorry.)

It was a proud day in Canadian history, when I stepped before the microphones in the Chateau Laurier hotel in Ottawa, and declared my candidacy for the leadership of the federal Liberal party. "I believe that I have the experience for the job, and the toughness to govern, tempered with compassion," I told the throng of press and well-wishers. How someone can be both tough and compassionate may surprise some people, but don't forget how I managed to balance the federal budget while building up huge deficits at the same time, back in the early 1970s. When you're a Liberal, everything is possible.

I had expected a coronation, but instead, it was a real fight. It took me two whole ballots to defeat my good friend and confidant, Jean Chrétien, who has done so much for me and the party, even to the point of resigning his seat and leaving politics. I hope.

I was sworn in as Prime Minister of Canada, on June 30, 1984, with 28 ministers surrounding me — down from the 36 of Trudeau. Look! Already I was showing the way with deep cuts and deflationary actions! I was advised by a number of people to put off facing the voters until late autumn, so that I could establish my own identity as Prime Minister, and have time to recruit a full slate of candidates to run in the West.

But there were so many excellent reasons for facing the voters at once! Moral reasons. Ethical reasons. And the real reasons, which were that we didn't want to get blamed for any economic downturn over the summer and fall, and that I had no seat in Parliament, and we were ahead of the Tories at that time, 48% to 39%.

So I hopped across the Atlantic and visited the Queen, requesting that she not come to Canada in July, as she had planned, so that we could have a summer campaign. And on July the 9th I asked the Governor-General to dissolve Parliament and set the election for that September the 4th.

And what happens even before I get my feet wet on the campaign trail? Pierre Trudeau, ever my nemesis, sticks me with seventeen expensive patronage appointments!

There were some other bad moments during that dreadful campaign, like when I said that Manitoba was losing population, when it was gaining, and when I patted some asses when I was gaining votes, and suddenly started losing. It's just so unfair, isn't it? God, but I miss the 40s and 50s, when men were boys, and girls were gals, and always the twain did meet.

We needn't discuss the fiasco of that September, except to say that the people of Canada made a terrible, terrible mistake, as they are quickly finding out. But I have a new job, now: to rebuild the Liberal party. And boy oh boy, is there a lot of rebuilding to be done. I can't believe that we lost Quebec. At least we never had the West, so that hurts less. There will be no back-stabbing in my party. No, I am dedicating the next few decades to covering this country, from coast to coast, visiting the public, discovering their wants and needs, and, along the way, bashing as many Tories as possible.

I can do it. I know I can. I was Prime Minister once, for a few precious weeks. I will be Prime Minister again, for a few glorious decades. I'm not even 60 yet; I've got lots of time. And lots of other things. Tenacity. Silver hair. Intelligence. Blue-grey eyes. Energy. A strong chin.

And a bright, attractive wife, and four bright, attractive children. And a group of excellent Liberal Members of Parliament, who will fight along next to me, to regain our rightful dominance as leaders of Canada.

It's true, I have recently lost my good friend Jean Chrétien, who has tragically decided to leave politics, so I will not have him next to me in the struggle. I guess I'll just have to manage without him. A-he-he-he-he-he. A-he-he-he-he-he-he. (Sorry.)

PIERRE MARC JOHNSON

When I was asked to write my autobiography, I thought they wanted to hear about my brilliant father Daniel Johnson, who was the Union Nationale Premier of Québec from 1966 until his death, two years later, and how he had inspired me.

I assumed that they wanted to hear about how I am both a doctor and a lawyer, which is certainly like billing two birds with one stone. Or is that stoning two birds with one bill?

I believed that they wanted to hear of my excellent cabinet ministries in the Parti Québécois government from 1977 to 1985, including Justice Minister.

I trusted that they wanted to know about my involvement in the ''associationniste'' group, as opposed to the ''separatiste'' faction, within the PQ.

I was sure that they wanted to know how I spearheaded the successful movement to convince René Lévesque to drop the independence option in the 1986 election.

Or, at the very least, they wanted to know about my silver-gray hair and my cute little beard.

But no. The publisher has just informed me that they want to know about my career as Premier of Québec, between my replacing René Lévesque, and my losing to Robert Bourassa.

What more can I say?

STERLING LYON

OK, OK. So I *fought* against the entrenchment of French-language services in Manitoba, as Opposition Leader in 1983.

OK, OK. So I nearly advocated civil disobedience if the Canadian Charter of Rights was approved back in 1980, when I was the Conservative Premier of the province.

OK, OK. So I *did* say that the Charter "disembowels" the British parliamentary system, and is republican "poison" that wouldn't be tolerated in Canada. I never did like *poisson*, anyway.

OK, OK. So I *was* sworn in as a member of the Manitoba Court of Appeal in December, 1986, where I now must *administer* that Charter.

But do you realize how *far* my $105,000 salary will *go* in Winnipeg in the latter half of the 1980s?

And really — stop to think about it for a damned second (and preferably in English, if you would): Who *wouldn't* sell out his or her principles for 105 Big Ones a year?

A hell of a lot of *women* sure would.

COLIN THATCHER

I have nothing to say until the appeal is heard. If you want to know anything, talk to my lawyer. Just one thing though: the past few years of my life have disproven one ancient Canadian myth. You don't have to be appointed to the Senate in order to be fixed for life.

BARBARA MCDOUGALL

*Dedicated to the memory of the Continental and North-
land banks. R.I.P.O.F.F.*

How did I know that those banks would fail? Am I my banker's
keeper? I guess I was, since I was the Minister of State for Finance.
But if I had any idea that those two lousy financial fiascos would
go bellyup, do you honestly think that I would pour a billion bucks
in public funds to keep them afloat? Do you actually believe that
I would risk my hard-earned reputation, trying to prop up two rapid-
ly sinking ships? Don't answer those questions; they are rhetorical.
Look it up; it starts with r-h-e-t, not r-e-t.

You don't need to know that much more about me than you have
already read in the obituaries for the Continental and Northland.
And I had nothing to do with their deaths, I swear. I had an alibi;
I was in Ottawa at the time. Yes — that could have been the problem; who on earth would think that bankers stuck way out in the
far west of Canada — or wherever the hell Alberta is — would know
how to run financial institutions? Everyone knows that you have
to be in Ottawa or Toronto, to run a bank properly. Correction;
make that Toronto.

And speaking of Toronto, that's where I was born 49 years ago,
the eldest of three sisters. One is a librarian today; the other, a journalist. I've made it clear to both of them that they should keep their
money in their mattresses until I can get the mess of Canadian banking cleaned up. Yes, women still have to do this kind of mopping
up after the garbage that men leave behind them.

I grew up in a family of women — my dad died when I was 12
— where we all learned how to do so-called "men's jobs," fixing
the plumbing, changing a tire, saving a bank. My dad's passing
forced my mother into a workplace that discriminated against
women in both pay and treatment, and it taught me an important
lesson: Men can be trusted about as far as you can throw them.
Fortunately, since I learned ju jitsu and wrestling as a young girl,
I could throw them extremely well. And far.

126

I had a number of false starts, not unlike the Canadian economy under the federal Liberal party. I began to study at the world-renowned and world-respected School of Architecture of the University of Toronto, now nearly defunct. I had some problems, since I couldn't draw. But, in retrospect, so what? I know a lot of bankers who can't add. So I switched to political science and economics, where I would still be able to design banks.

I was a popular and intelligent student, if I say so myself. I was the vice president of the U. of T. student council, yet the president at the time never really amounted to anything. He was Walter McLean, later Secretary of State.

I am ashamed to admit it, but my early political affiliation was Liberal. You see, my family had been involved with the Liberal party for over a century. But, thank God, there was some good sense there as well. On my father's side, my grandfather was a Conservative organizer in the east end of Toronto. And my mom was a close friend of Olive Diefenbaker.

I decided to run for office in the election after Joe Clark's victory in 1979, and expected to spend years working my way up to that far-off date. Then, the Tories were unceremoniously kicked out of office just a few months later, and I simply wasn't ready to make the move so quickly. Nor, as the 1980 election was to prove, were most of the people in the Conservative party.

So I got my feet wet in the political arena. Well, moist. I ran two election campaigns for David Crombie in Rosedale, and became the president of the Rosedale Progressive Conservative Association. I was so loyal to li'l Dave, I actually worked valiantly for him, in his fight for the leadership of the Conservatives. Talk about lost causes.

Now it was time for my big move. In 1983, over a year in advance, I began my long struggle for the PC nomination in the riding of St. Paul's. It was a dreadful problem to try and get the big shots in the riding to accept me. So I laid it all out for them. True, I told them; I lacked experience. I was too young. I was female. I'd never been elected to anything since the student council at the University of Toronto. But I was good!

I won the nomination, raised about 30 grand, and campaigned up to 16 hours a day, riding my bike across the huge riding, winning votes and respect from everyone. My opponent made it easy for me; his name was John Roberts, and although he was rather cute, and had a good brain, he was a Liberal, which pretty well did him in, even before he started campaigning. I beat him royally, which was just fine with me.

Oh, yes, I forgot to mention: during those missing years, when I wasn't in politics, I was a business journalist, a columnist for *Chatelaine*, a TV journalist in Edmonton, a vice-president at A.E. Ames and Co. Ltd. and Dominion Securities Ames Ltd., and executive director of the Canadian Council of Financial Analysts. But who cares. The real thing began in September, 1984. That was when the Grits hit the fan.

I was promptly given the role of junior finance minister, in the much-anticipated Progressive Conservative federal government, with the job of reforming our stupid financial system in Canada. Originally created by Ferdinand and Imelda Marcos, or so it seems, it had not been shaken up for quite a while, and it was my job to do it.

So, as fast as I could — April, 1985, to be exact — I put out a discussion paper on banks, insurance companies and other financial institutions. It was excellent. But then came the catastrophe(s). The Canadian Commercial Bank suffered a crisis. So I bailed it out. Then it collapsed, followed in quick succession by the Northland Bank. Thanks, guys.

Then, along came a minor crisis in the insurance industry, as the average cost of car insurance for a 24-year-old boy in Canada moved up a bit from $800 a year, to $43,000. Those punks drive like lunatics, you've got to admit. And then a number of insurance companies joined the Commercial and the Northland in that Great Bankruptcy World in the Sky.

As you can well imagine, the Grits jumped all over me in the House of Commons, but I could take it. I knew I was in the right. I explained calmly how I had studied the history of both banks carefully, and how impressed I was with their $23 billion worth of loans to Nicaragua, Haiti, the Philippines, and Colin Thatcher. I understood that it's not easy to second-guess the world's economies, and that the Commercial and the Northland tried their best. Of course, so did Baby Doc Duvalier.

But those reforms will come through, that I promise. The process is slower than I expected. In government, changes take legislation, and legislation takes time. And time, as we all know, takes money. Something I don't have much of, now that I've had to shell out all that cash to try to save the two western stinkers.

I have big plans for our banking system, or that which is left of it. I plan to beef up the powers of the inspector-general of banks, and the superintendent of insurance, with major, structural changes to the system. It won't be overnight. But then, Rome wasn't rebuilt in a day. Although to look at their ancient buildings today, you'd think it was.

Now, if Der Hoi Yin and the CBC would only lay off poor Eddie Kaiser and the Bank of British Columbia. . . .

Well, hallelujah! I'm finally out of the bank vaults and into the real world!! In the June, 1986, Cabinet shuffle, I was moved over to become Minister of State for Privatization and Minister responsible for the Status of Women. It's true, I *had* been asking for Trade, or Communications, or Consumer and Corporate Affairs, but this could be a lot of laughs, too. First, I get to try and dump Canadair, Eldorado Nuclear and Teleglobe. And second, I get to make Women Numero Uno, at least in Canada.

True, I'll have to deal with various Neanderthals in order to clean shop: Crosbie controls Air Canada and Canadian National, and he'll probably fight for their sick little lives. And Masse has Petro-Canada under his belt, and what lady would want to hit below there?

In a nutshell, I've got to somehow turn a lot of Crown Corps into Crown Corpses. But a girl who could talk her way out of Northland and Commercial can do pretty much anything.

129

JOE GHIZ

Dal? Harvard Law? Please don't mention them! I'm just Joe Ghiz, the Charlottetown-born kid, son of an immigrant from the Middle East, who used to work in daddy's grocery store after school, and who feels more at home in jeans and a sweater than a three-piece suit.

Now, I'm Premier of the smallest province with the largest name: Prince Edward Island. And I did it through honesty, decency, a good campaign, and, most important of all, destructive Tories in Ottawa, combined with self-destructive Tories in Charlottetown. Unlike in national politics, it pays to be a Liberal in P.E.I. Or, at least last April it did.

It wasn't that way back in 1982, just four years ago. That's when I ran my first campaign against Jim Lee's Tories, shortly after I had been elected provincial Liberal leader. He beat us badly — 21 seats to our 11. But just a few short years later, the numbers were exactly the same, but the winner and loser were reversed. Way ta go, Joe!!!

Boy was I mad back then! But it was my fault, in a way. I used too many five dollar words in a province where five bucks can buy you a downpayment on a potato farm. No, make that the first mortgage, and most of the second. Things have really been rather depressed out here.

What really hurt me, however, was that there was a fiasco of a Liberal government in Ottawa, which I'd just as soon not talk about. After what *they* had been doing to the economy, what chance would we P.E.I. Liberals have in getting the Islanders to vote Grit at home? About the same chance of getting a tourist to visit the Island in January, that's how much.

So I spent every single day and night over the last 48 months visiting every farmer, fisherman and tourist operator in the province. Fortunately, that's a lot easier than it sounds; the entire island is about the size of downtown Regina. Make that suburban Penetang.

I was also helped by Jim Lee, the Tory Premier, who I'm pretty sure wasn't too anxious to help me at all. Bland! Why, he made Bill Davis of Ontario look like Warren Beatty at an orgy. But if Lee was only bland, he'd have done alright. His ingenious shenanigans with the Prince Edward Island Hotel and Convention Centre couldn't have been any better for me, if I myself had planned them. And they often looked as if I had.

Oh, I was great! I fought him on the beaches. I fought him in the potato fields. I fought him on the streets of Sunnyside and Charlottetown. Now you know where Winston Churchill got all his greatest images from.

And I wiped the Tories out, as I said before, taking 21 of the province's 32 seats. I like to talk about it, so I don't mind repeating it.

The only really tense moment was when people kept talking about "the bigotry factor," which implied that some Islanders might not vote for me, because of my ethnic background. I thought at first that they were suggesting that I had come from the mainland, which is the kind of slur that no Islander could afford. But no, I was born in Charlottetown, so that couldn't have been it.

It ended up being about the fact that my father was born in Lebanon. But so what? The federal Tories are all from Hunger, and no one seems to care about *that*.

Anyway, I just pointed out to the press and public that I was proud of being a Canadian, proud of being an Islander, and proud of being of Lebanese extraction. And let's face it: If my dad could get out of Lebanon in one piece, he must have been pretty smart, right? How many others can make that claim?

I've got big plans now that I'm in power. Or, whatever power you can have in a province where getting 4,644 votes, as I did in Queens Sixth, is considered a landslide. I plan to bring in a denticare program — since you need good teeth to eat potatoes, and provide assistance for farmers, who are going under faster than you can say "Ghiz the Whiz." Which is damned fast.

All of this, along with pharmacare for senior citizens and a clothing allowance for people on welfare, is going to cost a bundle.

But so what? Fully half of Prince Edward Island's budget is met by transfer payments from the Feds. God bless those Tories in Ottawa; they not only got me elected, through their stupid increasing of use fees, potato inspection fees and wharfage fees on the Island, but they'll keep me in power through all those transfer bucks.

God, I love Canadian politics. Now, if I can only find out what the hell to do with that hotel and convention centre in downtown Charlottetown. . . . Maybe plant potatoes in the rooms? Hang fishing nets from the windows? If I could somehow get it shipped to my father's birthplace, it would probably be blown up within a week, and quickly forgotten.

Any suggestions? Just drop a note to the P.E.I. Assembly, Charlottetown, P.E.I.

C/O Ghiz. *Premier* Joe Ghiz. Formerly of Dalhousie and Harvard, but now A Man of the People, With Red Dirt Under His Nails and Transfer Payments in His Overalls. Which is what Canadian politics is all about. At least in the Maritimes. Where the least is the most we can ever expect.

Straight from the $800 Day

DONALD MACDONALD

I would have liked this autobiography to be a lot longer, but what could I do? Trudeau stuck me with that job, heading his Royal Commission on the Economy, in order to get me out of his hair.

It was a dirty trick, but it worked for Mulroney, when he sent Stephen Lewis down to the UN, taking him out of circulation as well.

So what does everyone talk about? My $800 a day fee. And the $925 a day, when I was on the road. But that's petty cash for the lawyers and businessmen I hang around with.

So because of that lousy commission, I'm *out* of commission.

That's the last time I listen to Pierre Trudeau. But then, all Canadians have the good fortune to be able to say that today, don't they?

ALLAN BLAKENEY

How can a 61-year-old politician who ran his province for nearly a dozen years be considered "old?"

Ronnie Reagan is young at 76, for crissake.

And how could Grant Devine claim that Tommy Douglas would have voted for him? Colin Thatcher, *maybe*, if they ever franchise prisoners.

Well, I've had it up to *here* with Saskatchewan voters. Divine Right may have worked for the French Kings, but the Devine Right was too left-wing for me to defeat.

You won't have me to mistreat any more; I'm getting my potash out of here.

DAVID PETERSON

Let's get this straight, now: *I* am the Premier of Ontario. I, David Peterson, with the beautiful actress wife and the beautiful active future, am the Liberal Premier of this great province. I, and not Bob Rae of the NDP, no matter how much he claims that he is. It's true, we have only 49 seats in the 125-seat Legislature, and that the Socialists' 25 seats have been rather helpful — more than helpful — in our gaining and retaining power. But I am the Premier, and not Rae.

Now that that is settled, let's take a look at my extraordinary career. Actually, let's take a look at my extraordinary few months in power, which amounts to the same thing.

You see, the last year or so has been a good time for me and the provincial Liberal party. Back in early May, 1985, when we went into an election against Frank Miller of the Tories, who had recently replaced Bill Davis, 7 out of 10 people in our province did not know who I was. And today, in the fall of 1986, 10 out of 10 people in the province want to re-elect my party to lead them into the 21st century. Or so it seems. Why, I even got to meet Charles and Di at Expo! That fact alone should help the few undecided to vote in our favour.

We can skip over my wealthy background in London, Ontario, and my long, painful wandering in the political desert of Ontario politics, searching for Liberal votes. We can skip over my gorgeous wife, and our picture-postcard children, and the fact that I can jog as well as any Yuppie. What really counts is this:

On June 18, 1985, the NDP joined with my Liberals to bounce out the Ontario Progressive Conservatives, who had been preserving it and conserving it for as long as I'd been on Earth. It was time, dear God; it was time.

It's true, we Liberals did have to sign a rather stringent agreement with Bob Rae, which I'd just as soon not discuss. But we got rid of the Tories, alright, and as every politician knows, the ends always justify the means. Or something to that effect.

I've often called myself "an accident of history," in that a whole lot of lucky things came together at just the right time: Davis's stepping down; a more right-wing successor replacing him; an Ontario public tired of Tory wishy-washness; a Tory government in Ottawa, making Ontarians anxious to balance that with a different government in Toronto; but most important of all, my new contact lenses, which make me look so much more attractive.

And what astonishing progress we have made, since I rose to the pinnacle of Ontario Power! I felt very comfortable, the very moment I sat down in the premier's office. So I immediately went ahead and stripped every single lawyer of the idiotic QC after his or her name, which has just about as much meaning as the letters MPP after a Tory politician in Ontario.

The lawyers were furious! But that was nothing, compared to the rage of the Ontario Medical Association, when I passed a bill to stop extra-billing by the province's doctors. They went on strike! Still, sticking it to the professionals didn't hurt my image with the public. Everyone hates doctors and lawyers.

The rest of my moves have been strongly social in nature, having little or nothing to do with the secret agreement with, and the threats from, Rae and the NDP. No, we Liberals have always wanted to reform tenant laws, fight for tougher environmental laws, improve safety in the workplace, push for pay equity between men and women, and extend separate school financing. Well, most of them, anyway.

There are still so many things to do! I've also promised to abolish Ontario Health Insurance Plan premiums, which place an unfair burden upon the poor and middle class, who have so many more votes than the rich. And I plan to bring in a denticare plan for children who have so many more teeth than the rich — and voting parents too.

My greatest promise, of course, and one which will have statues of me on every corner of every street in the province of Ontario, is my desire to sell beer and wine on the corner of every street in the province of Ontario.

How can I explain how important this is, to the future of our province? How can I tell you how mortifying it has been in the past, not be able to pick up a six pack with each visit to the neighborhood Mac's or Becker's?

We Liberals will make every 7-11 a place for you! We'd prefer if you didn't drive there, and left the car at home, but there are other laws that cover that, I assure you.

Have I made any mistakes in my fantastic year and a half at the top of Ontario politics? To be honest about it, I occasionally say things that I later regret, such as when I said that there are too many doctors in Ontario, and that it might be a good idea to impose a health-care tax on higher-income Ontarians. But what man hasn't said something that he later regrets? Of course, what man has two dozen nosey reporters following him around, every single minute of every single day? And I'm getting sick and tired of it, too. Journalists could be the next group to have their earnings regulated, if they don't watch their step around me.

No, it's the beginning of a new era for the province of Ontario! No more bland; lots more grand. We are giving the people of my province what they have longed for over the past four decades, but could never get with the Tories in power: Consumer-oriented legislation. Interventionism. Lawyer and doctor bashing. And lots of free spending.

In the next election, which I can call whenever I bloody well please, in spite of my so-called Accord with the Socialists, I plan to demolish the NDP, and Larry Grossman of the Tories as well.

It's a new dynasty for Ontario. The NDPs and the PCs are about to be thrown out, along with the QCs and the MDs. All this, along with beer and wine sitting next to the milk, eggs and dirty mags. Yes, Nirvana has finally come to our richest and most populous province, and it came wrapped in Liberal colours. In a few more years, I won't even have to legislate the wearing of red ties to all public events; people will do it naturally; without thinking. Kind of like the way they used to vote for the Progressive Conservatives in Ontario.

And they'll vote for me. Me. David Peterson. The leader of the Liberal party of Ontario.

*OK with you,
Mr. Rae? Dave*

JOHN GAMBLE

I was proud to serve as a lawyer in Markham, Ontario.

I was proud to serve as Member of Parliament for York North.

I was proud to run for the head òf the federal Progressive Conservatives.

I was proud to run for cover, after having been dumped on the first ballot.

But what could be the cause of more pride than to be the Chairman of the North American region of the World Anti-Communist League, and raise millions for the Contras of Nicaragua?

And being a true, passionate Canadian, what could be more logical than to follow in the footsteps of the True Oliver North, Proud and Free?

KENNETH DYE

Can't these buggers *add*?

41 million smackers wasted, by putting that prison into Mulroney's riding way up in Port-Cartier!

Unavailable documents on Petro-Canada's purchase of Petrofina!

The CBC's not knowing its financial acts from a hole in the ground!

No *wonder* the Feds — whether Tory or Grit — keep running around promising to "never say Dye." They can't afford to admit I *exist*.

But then, the rest of Canada can't afford to let *them* exist, either.

Who says that crime doesn't pay?

RENÉ LÉVESQUE

[Reluctantly translated from the Français]

I personally can't understand why you readers out there couldn't take the trouble to learn French, in order to read my story in the original. After all, French is one of the two official languages of the country of Canada. In fact, French is the only official language of the country of Quebec and my Parti Québécois, who taught the Anglos such phrases as *À VENDRE*, which they promptly placed in front of their palatial homes, right across the western suburbs of Montreal. But that is more recent; if you want me to tell my whole story, then I should perhaps start at the beginning — or, as Quebec children of every race, color and belief are wont to say "at le start."

I was born in 1922, on the south shore of the Gaspé peninsula, where the French-speaking natives of our country had been pushed by the ever-advancing hordes of England, Scotland and Ireland. I was the oldest and tallest of four, born to a lawyer and his appendage and had a Jesuit education, given by priests who had been crushed by centuries of oppression from an Italian-speaking Church.

I went off to Laval University in Quebec City where I earned a BA degree. I was briefly in law school, until I was kicked out by a future Supreme Court Justice, Louis-Phillippe Pigeon — for smoking. Even from my earliest years, I was associated with the best of people: Jesuit priests. Law professors. Marlboro Men.

My first job was that of announcer and editor of the Nouveau — then New — Carlisle radio station, CHNC. Indeed, even while at Laval, I earned pocket money by doing the announcing for a Quebec City station, CHRC. I was a born communicator, as is well known. I was also a knock-out poker player, but that's another matter.

I went overseas, as a French-language expert for the Psychological Warfare Bureau of the American armed forces. I would use my knowledge of psychological warfare in my later years as a politician. I did broadcast reports for the CBC, as well. I saw the bombing of London and the opening of Dachau, and picked up some great ideas for the future.

Right through 1944, I was with the Yankee troops, as they pushed back the Nazis, preparing my very special reports for the military. The fools couldn't understand a single word, unfortunately. I'm really quite fond of the Yanks, but they can't speak or read French worth a goddam, anymore than the average Anglo-Canadian.

I then spent a year as an announcer in the French-language section of the CBC International Service, and for the next five years, I was chief of the CBC's French network news service. I covered the visit to Canada of Prince whatshisface and Princess whateverhernameis, of England, and the glorious visitation of Vincent Auriol, the President of France. What touched me most, in those years, I must admit, was covering the Korean War for the CBC; it was deeply moving and inspiring for me to witness Sovereignty-Association work so well in another land.

From 1958 until I finally entered politics, my handsome visage and statuesque physique — ever notice how many hundreds of thousands of French words have entered the English language? — were seen regularly on French language television, right across Quebec.

So you can readily comprehend why Jean Lesage looked to me as a kind of saviour, when he began to push the Union Nationale out of power. I was the candidate in the Montreal constituency of Laurier, named after the great French-speaking Prime Minister from earlier in this century. My UN opponent fought dirty, as one would expect, but I still won by nearly 5,000 votes in the 1960 election. And I won again, three years later.

Premier Lesage wisely chose me as Minister of Public Works and Hydraulic Resources, and, soon after, as Minister of Natural Resources. And with a natural resource like me, how could they lose? I nationalized Hydro Quebec, even if that scum Bourassa keeps trying to take all the credit today. I always speak well of the dead, but the resurrected will have to fend for themselves.

I had decided to do nothing less than rebuild the great province and future country of Quebec from the ground up. And since the French-speaking majority of my province had all been squashed to the ground by the English-speaking minority, I had a lot of supporters all over the ground, just waiting to join me. We would create a New Quebec: Culturally. Socially. Intellectually. Economically.

None of this so-called co-operative federalism jazz; I know very well how the system in South Africa works. And the whites just love it.

As the years passed, I began to get a reputation as a leftist in the Liberal party. I can't imagine why; after all, did I not break all those strikes in 1983, when I was in power? Well, anyway, the Liberals were defeated in 1966, and I tried to make the party more nationalistic, but they just wouldn't budge. So I founded a superb new political entity, the Parti Québécois, in 1968. We separatists were united at last!

It was not all roses, at first. We lost in 1970, and we lost in 1973, but it would only be a matter of time until the majority of Québécois began to see the light. And in 1976, it happened: the Parti Québécois came to power! At last, we would show les maudit Anglais who was le boss! At last, we would prove that we Francophones could be masters of our own house!!

And we did, mon Dieu, we did. Do you know that in the 1960s, over 90% of all immigrants attended English schools!! But why? The French were in the majority, weren't they? And the year we came to power, only about a dozen of the 100 biggest businesses in Quebec operated in French! Hey — I just realized! Maybe that is why all the immigrants wanted to study English! Now I get it! Of course! Why didn't I realize that before!?

Anyway, they wouldn't get the choice, once we got elected. That's because we pushed through Bill 101, which was a lot like Bill 22 of the hated Bourassa Liberals, but, as the number says, about five times more powerful. Oh, it was stupendous! We forced all future immigrants to study in French schools! We made French the only language of the courts! Streetsigns and advertising had to be in French! Yes, French was, at last, becoming the language of most businesses!

But our greatest move was toward Sovereignty-Association, which we saw as the ultimate solution to the millennia-old frustration of Quebec's constitutional rights. True, more than 130,000 English-speaking Quebeckers left the province, between 1976 and 1981, but who needed them? They were only taking jobs away from francophones anyway. There was a Referendum, which I'd rather not talk about, since the English-speakers must have voted two and three times each, and a fair number of French-speakers just didn't seem to have the brains to understand what I was getting at.

142

Look, we were re-elected again, weren't we? I must admit, though, the last few years have not been too pleasant. Hundreds of thousands of young people could not find jobs, probably because women kept taking them away from the men who have to work. The Canadian Constitution was patriated, and without a Quebec veto, which is one of the stupidest things I've ever heard of; I'm still not sure how that happened. Then there was that lousy public sector workers strike. And, if all this weren't enough, I found that I was spending most of my time arranging bail for my Cabinet ministers. (One probably forgot that he was wearing the coat, and those little girls, I am sure, seduced the other guy. They can be very seductive, you know). Sure our Quebec taxes are high, and the bureaucracy is huge, but those sort of things just happen, when you run a government.

Oh, my enemies have been hard on me, and it's just not fair! "The Little Dictator," they call me. What a laugh. I'm not so small; in fact, I'm a full half-inch taller than Woody Allen, and he always ends up getting the girl. And the great Gilles Vigneault wrote his song, *"Gens du Pays"* in honour of me and the Parti Québécois.

Anyway, I stepped down, and let Pierre-Marc Johnson take over as head of my beloved, unfairly persecuted party. Johnson!! What a silly name; it hardly sounds French. And a doctor and a lawyer at the same time? What does he do, sue himself for malpractice?

So we lost the last election. And to Bourassa, who I was just sure was dead. But I know that in their hearts, the people still want and love the Parti Québécois, and they want to be independent, to be free, to be separatist. I, personally, am a Liberal at heart, so I guess my heart just wasn't in it, at the end. But I haven't turned my back on my beloved province! Do you realize how much money I gave to the people of Quebec, in cigarette taxes, during the few hours it took me to write this autobiography? A goddamn fortune! And if you were to add up all the cigarette tax money that I've given to the country/province of Quebec over the past half-century, it could pay all the overdue bills of the Montreal Olympics.

I'm retired now, and independence for Quebec has been put on the back burner, as the bastards say in English. My only regret is, I've never been able to figure out what the hell "Sovereignty-Association" means. If anyone knows, please write to me, care of this publisher. And in French, dammit.

Straight from the Patronage

BRYCE MACKASEY

Dear Fitzhenry & Whiteside:

I'm sorry that I've been unable to get my autobiography in on time for your publication date. I realize that we had a written contract, but then, so did I, with Trudeau and Turner. You, like Portugal, will have to wait.

Sincerely yours,

Bryce Mackasey

Please. *You* tell *me*: what the hell can a little visit to a bar and strip joint in West Germany have to do with jeopardizing Canadian security? Since when has Canada had any secrets to give out, much less to keep? That Wayne Gretzky is from Brantford, and not Edmonton? That Joe Clark is Catholic?

Sure, I was the Defence Minister, and sure, the stripper was born in East Germany, but so what? At least she spoke understandable English, which is more than you can say about John Crosbie.

Anyway, it's true that there was nude dancing, and dirty movies, but if that's all I was interested in, I could always hop over to Hull, which is just minutes from Parliament.

BUT I DID NOT OFFER MY RESIGNATION, AND BRIAN DID NOT ASK FOR IT. AND THAT'S THE TRUTH.

And about that stripper, Miss Micki O'Neil: she was a pretty good dancer, which is more than you could say about anyone in the Tory caucus.

And it's simply a bare-faced lie that I told Miss O'Neil I was travelling to Ankara the next day. Hell, I don't even know where Ankara is. And what if I did tell her where I was travelling the next day? Would this have led to the fall of the Western Alliance? Would Canada have had to pull out of NATO? Would the U.S.S.R. have refused to pull out of Afghanistan? I certainly didn't see anyone pull out of anyone in those movies they were showing in that bar; that's for damn sure.

Anyway, I got kicked out of Mulroney's Cabinet. But every cloud has a silver lining. In fact, I believe that Ms. O'Neil's G-string had a silver lining.

And what's the happy side of all this? I've got a libel case going against the Ottawa Citizen, which could land me a pretty penny. And then I could travel to West Germany any time I wanted, and no one would bother me.

Not only that, but the next time I visit a nudie bar, at least I won't be risking the future of Western Civilization. It would be just too much of a responsibility to bear.

Straight from the Blessed Peacemakers

STEPHEN LEWIS

You win, Brian. You cut out my tongue, by making me an offer that I couldn't refuse, something that I had always thought was more Italian than Irish. I can't criticize your actions up in Canada, since I'm too busy getting the Russians out of Afghanistan, the whites out of South Africa, and the Libyans out of airports.

Just a question to the publishers of this book: If you talk with Brian — he never returns my calls — would you be so kind as to find out why he's less anxious to have me get the Americans out of Nicaragua?

HARVIE ANDRE

We've offered you things that no other business in Canada would ever even THINK of offering you:
— LESS SERVICE FOR MORE MONEY!

That's right, everyone! For barely 5% more than you are paying now for a first-class stamp, you can have:
— DOWNGRADED MAIL DELIVERY STANDARDS!

— SUPERMAILBOXES, instead of that old-fashioned door-to-door delivery, which even your grandparents used to get!!

— HUNDREDS OF RURAL POST OFFICES CLOSED IN THE BLINK OF AN EYE!

Now, be honest: Could any other firm in Canada make such an offer, and even *hope* to stay in business?

Not on your life!

So wish me well in my new role as the head of Canada Post, which has just been added to my Consumer and Corporate Affairs portfolio.

But please don't *mail* me your congratulations; use a courier service. I'd really like to be *sure* of getting your cards and letters.

Thanks.

Harv

Straight from the Bland

WILLIAM DAVIS

People often mocked me for taking polls before deciding any important action on the part of my government. This, in fact, was not so. I took polls before deciding *any* action, important or unimportant, on the part of *anything* I've done in my life. Indeed, it's been correctly declared that I've taken more polls than the Germans and the Russians.

Take, for instance, the poll I took before deciding to write my autobiography. It was a private and personal poll, true, but a poll, nonetheless. My wife Kathleen thought that it would be a good idea, in that I'd get the opportunity to express my feelings about my political career. So that was One For. Our daughter Meg, on the other hand, thought that "anything I say could be used against me," which sounds like she's been watching too many American cops and robbers shows, but anyway, that made One Against.

The other four children, Neil, Nancy, Katherine and Ian, split right down the middle, making it Three For and Three Against. Which left me in a real dilemma, one which I just hate. Now I might actually have to make a decision! So I turned to my spiritual adviser and Cardinal Carter said: DO IT.

I was born in the summer of 1929, shortly before the Great Depression which would so damage our Canadian way of life and crush our economy. It didn't hurt my family so much, however, since my dad was a lawyer. And lawyers can make a good living anywhere, even in a small town like Brampton, Ontario.

Brampton, just 20 miles northwest of Toronto, used to be called "the flower capital of Canada," but the place was really Tory City, with babies who showed Grit or NDP leanings being left on the side of Main Street to bloom for themselves. My dad was a Crown Attorney and a Conservative of the Old School. Why, his best buddy was Tom Kennedy, who was briefly Premier of Ontario. So it was only natural that I would follow the proper path to Righteousness and Power — which are, as we all know, synonymous.

I attended the public elementary and secondary schools of Brampton — no fancy, hi-falutin' private Liberal schools for me! I even quarterbacked for Brampton High. A lot of my best buddies were Catholic, and I thought it was a shame that they couldn't continue their parochial education through grade 12. I was never a terribly good law student, and vowed, even at that young age, to make the schools a lot easier, so anyone could do well. And in later years, as Education Minister of the Province of Ontario, I did just that.

Since law was a pre-requisite for a political career in Ontario at that time, I moved on to the University of Toronto. I played intermediate intercollegiate football — note the word "intermediate", which would describe my entire career in the future — and my Number 71 Jersey still hangs proudly in my closet. In point of fact, I'm wearing it now, as I am dictating this, in my Georgian Bay cottage.

After I managed to complete my BA degree, in 1951, I moved on to Osgoode Hall Law School, where I received my LLB degree, four years later. Then, after searching around for a job, I returned to Brampton and became a partner in daddy's law firm.

But politics was always my goal; the polls told me that in an instant. When I was only 16, back in 1945, I was actually a delegate to the national convention of the Progressive Conservatives. And just four years later, still too young to vote, I won the presidency of the Progressive Conservative Association of Peel Riding, where I lived. I was quite a whiz kid.

After that it was just one poll, or rather, one honour after another. I became the Tory MPP for Peel Riding, and my rise was meteoric! First, I was chosen as the second vice-chairman of Ontario Hydro, which just happens to run the province. And then, in late October, 1962, Robarts gave me the education portfolio!

The voters, of course, were suitably impressed. So when I ran again, in the election that following year, I won with a hefty majority. And an election is the Ultimate Poll. But then, so is Pope John Paul II.

Soon I took on the dual appointment of Minister of Education as well as University Affairs, and made huge changes in the education system of Ontario:

— I cut the number of school boards in the province from more than 5,000, down to 150. I never liked addition, anyway.

— Bigger, central schools were created out of many rural schools. I always was a centralist.

— I created educational television, so people across the province could spend Saturday night watching black-and-white 'B' movies from the 1930s.

— I built dozens of colleges of applied arts and technology across the province, for all those people who didn't have daddy's business to go into, and didn't want to go to university.

— And, most inspired of all, I modernized the curriculum! Now, how can I explain this simply enough so that people who have graduated from Ontario schools since the mid-60s will understand?

You see, there was this study, the Hall-Dennis report, which basically said that schools had become a drag, what with the 3Rs and all. So I began to order a much greater latitude in the choice of subjects to be studied by our young people. Give 'em a break! Especially the Catholics!

For instance, if the students thought English was the pits, they would be allowed to take a suitable related alternative, such as *Pop Music Lyrics, 101*. And if they just couldn't tell an accent ague from an accent grave, then they would be allowed to study *Slang In Contemporary Life, 409*. Was Geometry too hard? Why not *Learning to Use A Calculator, 313*? And if Art was a toughie, there was always *Paint By Numbers, 294*. School began to be fun, entertaining, even joyous, for the students. And the teachers loved it too, since there were few, if any, papers to mark. I was amazing! I visited schools, spoke to student groups, parent groups, teacher groups — and they all loved me, because I used simple, one-syllable words, and waved my hands a lot.

Now that I had devastated education, my political ambitions began to extend beyond the Cabinet. In 1970, John Robarts decided to step down, and I quickly threw my hat into the ring. (For recent graduates of Ontario schools, I'd better explain that: throwing your hat into the ring is a metaphor. It means, I declared my interest in winning the position. What's a metaphor . . . ?)

It was another tough campaign. I ran, against five other candidates, on my record of making the Ontario educational system one of the most effective in North America. It was a close vote, but on February 13, 1971, I defeated the others, and on March 1st, I was sworn in as the 18th Premier of the Magnificent Province of Ontario. I quickly turned to the voters of the province, most of whom could still read a simple, five letter word like D-A-V-I-S, and would have little or no trouble with a four letter word like T-O-R-Y, and most certainly they'd recognize a two letter abbreviation like P-C, and called an election for October, 1971.

It wasn't all roses, but I managed to keep the Big Blue machine going for thirteen more years, even though we did hit some rocky spots. And I discovered something amazing. Bland works: and the bland leading the bland, or, in other words, the Tories leading the people of Ontario, is precisely what everyone wanted.

Throughout my tenure as Premier of Ontario, I maintained my integrity and my ambiguity. I argued against making Ontario officially bi-lingual while slowly extending new rights to Franco-Ontarians through provincial legislation. I took polls on day care, topless dancing, and all those other things that Ontarians feel strongly about, and then acted accordingly. Or didn't act. Whatever they wanted was fine with me.

Of course you can't satisfy everyone all the time. There was the abortion issue — I don't want to talk about it! And there was the Spadina Expressway — I don't want to talk about that either! But by and large I did it. And by the end of 1984, I had tired of having to make all those decisions, decisions, decisions. I was tired of the endless polls: Should I get up at 7 a.m. or 8 a.m.? Should I brush my teeth? Should I show my teeth when I smile? Should I take a poll on taking another poll, or would that be wise? Maybe I should take another poll on whether I should take a poll on taking polls? Or maybe not? You can't imagine what it was like!

So I handed the job over to Frank Miller on February 8, 1985, and finally decided to leave public life, accepting a modest position with the aptly-named law firm of Tory, Tory, Deslauriers and Binnington. But even law could not satisfy my eager, searching mind. So I joined the boards of the Canadian Imperial Bank of Commerce, Ford Motor Company, Magna International, Honeywell Inc., Power Corporation, Seagram's Ltd., First Boston Canada Ltd., Nike Canada and Lawson-Mardon Group. Lots of fun and no decisions.

Anyway, that's my life until now. I've tried to avoid the more boring aspects of my career, such as acid rain. What's most important is that I am still alive and healthy, in my late 50s; that I've got a lovely wife and five bright kids. I can still boat, play softball and touch football, and can escape to Florida as often as I can get away.

151

Unless, of course, you think that a man my age shouldn't be playing such rough sports? Do you really think not? Maybe you're right. I'll get back to you, as soon as I can, on what I've decided.

Or haven't.

I think.

ANDRÉE CHAMPAGNE

I've been ordered by Mr. Mulroney never to put anything down in writing ever again.

Straight from the Nursery

WILLIAM VANDER ZALM

Are you kids ready? In your nighty-night clothes with your teeth all brushed? Wooden shoes all placed neatly under your beds?

Okay, then. *Here goes!!!*

Once upon a time, there was a wonderfully handsome prince, born in a faraway town called Noordwykerhout, in a Nether Land. It was a hard, difficult childhood, since there was an evil invading force from a nearby country, the Nasties, who stomped on flower beds and did other awful things.

Well, a Kingdom from across the sea, Canada, came and rescued the young prince, along with his homeland, and the prince — we'll call him Bill, okay? — the prince made a vow then and there that he would pay that country back for saving his country from the rotten Nasties. Yes, he would save that cold, forbidding, faraway country *from itself*.

So Prince Bill went off to a lotus land called British Columbia, in the western-most part of that country which had so generously taken the trouble to save his own, and joined his father, who had been smart enough to get out of the Nether Land while the getting was still good.

Handsome young Bill didn't tell anyone that he was a Prince — *they would discover that soon enough, kids!* — when he attended school in a town called Abbotsford. He didn't even learn English until he was in his early teens — but that didn't bother Bill! Later in life, he would meet grown-ups like Robert Skelly, who couldn't speak English in their 40s!!

When he was still just a barely pubescent lad, young Bill began to use the magic that he brought with him from his native Nether Land: He could make flowers and bushes grow from just little seeds! (Making money grow from trees would take a little longer.)

He was a kindly man, this Bill — he wouldn't even harm a fly, much less pull its wings off. And no sooner did he begin to work his magic on flowers, than he worked his magic on a lovely little girl named Lillian, who was as beautiful as she was financially

154

astute. She wore a magic sweatband, which the Prince was afraid to ask about, except that she could *never take it off*. (She once told Bill that, as long as she wore the sweatband, neither she nor anyone that she loved would ever grow old. And as of early 1987, it was still true.)

Even though Prince Bill (and Princess Lillian) had such a magic touch with flowers and eternal life, not to mention flies, which will remain untouched as long as Bill will be in office, he was soon attracted to POWER. He served as an alderman, and later as a mayor of a town near the magical city of Vancouver. It was because of his magical leadership that the town became known as ''Surrey with the Fringe at the Top.''

Later, while still a young man — *but he would remain eternally young, do remember!* — he performed his first political miracle! While the entire country of Canada went crazy in 1968 over a rather silly frog who never *could* turn into a prince, Bill ran as a federal Liberal and *still* managed to be defeated. Now *that* was *magic!*

A few years later, Prince Bill ran for the leadership of the Liberal Party in his beloved chosen province of British Columbia and was once again defeated! (This was no miracle, I can assure you. But it's not surprising that the people did not elect Prince Bill; as we know from countless other fairy tales, the common folk rarely recognize Beauty or Truth when they see it, even if it's wearing a sweatband.)

Then, another Prince (who had inherited *his* magic from his Father, the King) also named Bill, invited *Our* Bill to join his party, which was slightly to the right of Attila the Hun. Swept into major office for the first time in his magical career, Prince Bill was given the Human Resources portfolio, which was a wondrous thing to have: As a man who had been wealthy since his teens, who knew handicaps only from horses, and would never be elderly (*thanks to his wife's sweatband, remember!*), he wasn't sure what he was supposed to do. But it was all good fun, as was his playing at Municipal Affairs and Education.

Then, when the other Prince stepped down, Prince Bill had already learned the most important lesson in the world of POWER, at least in British Columbia: *Style is substance*. Remember that, kids, if you ever want to win big in that province.

And in the winter of 1986, the people finally brought Magic into their lives by electing Prince Bill their leader by a score of 49 to 20. Even though the unemployment rate was well over 12 percent, he immediately gave the people what they really needed to drown their sorrows: He raised the minimum wage from $3.65 to $4.00, and lowered the price of beer, so they could afford more.

But POWER was not what was *really* important to Prince Bill! No, MONEY was also nice. Over the years, he had taken his small nursery and show garden and turned it into what Canada needed most: A multi-million dollar theme park, with a petting zoo, a train ride, a Biblical garden, a theatre, a stocked trout lake, and much, much more. And he did it all for only $1.7 million on prime agricultural land, and there's so little of it left in British Columbia, too! But who knows more about land and its usage than Prince Bill, the Magician of the Garden?

No, Prince Bill has all the answers, and now that he is in POWER, with lots of MONEY, he can provide them for *everyone*, with his own monthly, hour-long talk show, PREMIER TALK, on CKNW radio. Who cares if chub-chub Dave Barrett was paid a fortune to have his own daily show? Socialists need money badly, in order to fund all their stupid political ideas, whereas Social Credit gets all the credit it needs, due to its "ins" with the banks!

Why, Prince Bill even has his own gardening video! He doesn't let little Opposition politicians bug him, when he's far more concerned about the bugs in our gardens!!

And then, in 1987, the little boy from the Nether Land would star in his own TV show, *Sinterklaas Fantasy*, riding a magical rainbow from Fantasy Gardens in his beloved British Columbia to his former home and native land!

Now, children, riding a magical rainbow half-way across the world might sound a bit scarey to you, but it *shouldn't* be! If the third most-populous province in Canada can accept style as substance, then why couldn't a Prince ride a rainbow? It's even *more* safe, and since Bill lands smack into a canal, why should the citizens of British Columbia expect anything any different?

Now, right off to bed, kids! I promised you one story, and you got it! You *do* believe it, don't you?

Don't you?

Straight from the PCs — Or is That NDP?

ROBERT TOUPIN

I never was happy with the Tories, to be honest about it — which already would make me a lousy Tory, wouldn't it? And when the SOBs had the gall to allow the closing of the Gulf Canada refinery in the east end of Montreal, that pretty well was the straw that broke this mammal's back.

And then I was basically told, "You can't quit; we fire you," by the idiots who run my riding of Terrebonne, near Montreal. So what could I do? I could either remain an Independent, which I had already become, or move (very) slightly to the left and join the Socialists.

Thank heavens, in this country, to move from the PCs to the NDP isn't a very far jump, as the *Toronto Sun* will tell you every other day.

So after a few top-secret meetings with Ed Broadbent, and a three-hour grilling by the executive of the Quebec wing of the NDP (some wanted me grilled well-done; others, rare), I was finally accepted.

This makes me the first-ever NDP member in Quebec, which is like being an elected black in South Africa. But then, what's the big deal? I'm old enough to remember when Quebec didn't have any PC members, either.

Basically, it comes down to one thing: We Québécois would rather switch than fight.

BILLY JOE MACLEAN

Who ran a hot dog stand beside the only movie house in Port
Hawkesbury?

BILLY JOE MACLEAN!

Who put up the first tavern ever built in Port Hawkesbury?

BILLY JOE MACLEAN!

Who managed to get the first high school put up in Port
Hawkesbury?

BILLY JOE MACLEAN!

Who brought in the first shopping mall in Port Hawkesbury?

BILLY JOE MACLEAN!

Who got the first nautical centre built in Port Hawkesbury?

BILLY JOE MACLEAN!

Who was the first member of the Nova Scotia assembly in 228
years to be indicted for a criminal offence?

BILLY JOE MACLEAN!

But before you get the wrong idea, let me tell you that purportedly
falsifying expense accounts to the amount of nearly $22,000 is no
big thing; most Newfoundlanders get that much in pogie every few
months.

And anyway, I wasn't sent to jail for 14 years, and was only fined
$6,000, but let me tell you, I was sure punished in other ways: I
was thrown to the wolves by the Progressive Conservative caucus,
ostracized by my fellow MPPs, and was even turfed out of the
Legislature!

Now is *that fair*? True, I'm pretty sloppy when it comes to book-
keeping, but just look at what the Auditor-General keeps coming
up with when he does Ottawa's books, and you'll start seeing the
unfairness of all this.

Of course, when my former buddy John Buchanan called a special
sitting of the Nova Scotia Legislature to pass a single bill strictly
in my honour — "to prohibit criminals from serving in the
Legislature," I began to see that this whole thing was being taken
rather seriously. But then, Buchanan *did* cry when I got tossed, so
how could I complain?

Still, I was vindicated in January of this year, when Chief Justice Madame Constance Glube decided that the buggers contravened the Charter of Rights when they forbade me from running again for a seat in the Legislature for another five years. True, she said they had the right to *toss* me out, but they couldn't *keep* me out!

Well, I'm back, thanks to the by-election in late February of '87. The people of Port Hawkesbury know that I may be a lousy book-keeper, but I'm one of the sweetest guys on the island of Cape Breton.

I may have to give up the Mercedes, though, because of all the ambulance-chaser fees. You know, maybe I should have become a lawyer instead of tavern-owner; if I had, I could have afforded an accountant to take care of my receipts, and this never would have happened.

Anyway, see you in the Nova Scotia Legislature!

You just can't keep a good guy down.

JOHN NUNZIATA

Why is everyone always so mad at me? Why is everyone so scared of me? Even when I was serving on the York municipal council in suburban Toronto, some eight years ago, I was called "the most disliked alderman." I was an NDPer back then; no wonder they hated me. But I'm a Liberal now — and a Member of Parliament, as well. So why does everyone wish I'd just go away?

But I won't go away, dammit. And that's a promise. I'm a big boy, now. Hell, I'm already over 30, which should make me pretty mature, right? Right?

Well, I think so, anyway. I mean, I'm a member of the Rat Pack, you know; those loud, muck-raking, passionate Liberal MPs who want to kick some Tory ass in Parliament. Everyone seems to love Sheila Copps, who has a voice like Dennis the Menace. And they all get a kick out of Don Boudria, who's more obsessed with patronage than Ronald Reagan with Muammar Khaddafi. So why don't they love me?

They call me "The Angry Young Man" of Parliament. But what the f--- is that supposed to mean? Only a dead man would be tolerant of these incompetent idiots in power, and I'm not dead yet.

Dammit, I thought that John Turner and the federal Liberals would be ecstatic to have a guy like me as a backbencher! Someone articulate who would attack the Tories every day in Question Period, who would challenge every stupid move they made.

So what does Ol' Blue Eyes do? He gets cold feet. Or as cold as feet can get, when they are sitting in his mouth all the time.

Turner seemed to enjoy Sheila, Don and me for a while. But then he began to get tired of our Rat Pack scurries in Parliament, and hinted that we were jeopardizing the credibility of the federal Liberal party. But what credibility, Johnny boy? When you've only got 40 seats in Parliament how can you have any credibility at all?

Okay, okay, so Johnny wanted us to do a bit more research, before we went in with guns blazing. Well we did, and we still can't get no respect.

Take last October, for instance. There I was, screaming at John Bosley, the Speaker of the House. And my Lord and Master John Turner speaks up. Thank the Lord, I think to myself. J.C. (Oh! I mean J.T.) is finally coming to my rescue. But no; what does he do? He has me rushed out of the Commons, like some drunk at one of his classy Rosedale parties.

You can imagine how I felt. Here I am, the Great Hope of the Liberal party, and they're too gutless to use me. Tuned-out Turner never seems to want me to ask anything during Question Period. And he refused to speak at my fundraiser last May in York South-Weston. But what finally broke this camel's back was when he passed me over as foreign affairs critic. And who does J.T. give the position to, but Don Johnston, who had just badmouthed Turner in his recent book!!

Anyway, I couldn't take it any more. So last April, I announced that the federal Liberal party should hold a full-fledged leadership convention that fall, instead of merely a vote of confidence in John Turner. I wanted to clear the air. And what happened? Everyone was mad at me again. Everyone was screaming at me.

All I wanted to do was prove to the country that Turner had every Liberal's support. But no one believed me. Everyone thinks that I was trying to stab John Turner in the back. Why doesn't anybody trust me?

So that's the way things stand now. Some of the Top Grits want to see me stripped of my job as watchdog on police activities. Others want me to apologize.

But why should I apologize? I'm John Nunziata! The Biggest Rat in the pack. And I swear, right here in print, that I am behind John Turner, all the way. Right behind him.

PIERRE TRUDEAU

(written in flawless English et Français)

The rose in my lapel is still there, and it's as fresh as ever. It's not frozen, zap or otherwise, like those wage and price controls which I fought against, but reluctantly had to impose after much consideration. I'm not wearing capes and buckskin jackets anymore, and the sandals are gone too. Not because I've outgrown them, but there's a dress code in this law office where I work now. Fortunately, Mercedes — the car, not the girl — are *de rigueur*.

I've stepped down from the dizzying heights of power in Ottawa, and I'm sure that every reader will agree, Canada — and the World, to which I brought eternal peace back in '83, will never be the same again.

The Canadian people were right to love me; they wanted a philosopher king and they got both: a man filled with ideas who ruled almost forever. I gave them what they wanted: TV in the House of Commons. Less foreign ownership. A lowered voting age. More opportunities for youth.

I also gave them what I wanted: Recognition of the Vatican and China. Bilingualism, biculturalism and bisexuality, the latter through my reform of the Criminal Code. The NEP. Less access to utterly unnecessary government information. Bannister slides. Queenly pirouettes. Movie star girlfriends. 465 obnoxious Quebecois arrested and held without bail. Actually, the latter was wanted by the Canadian people, as well.

Most important, I was described in the London *Daily Sketch* as "the world's seventh sexiest man." Just so long as the six before me were not in Canadian politics, why should I care? (Shrug)

Do you not recall that Senator Mondale once declared that "Pierre Trudeau is a priceless asset to the industrialized world"? Whether he meant that no one could afford me, I'm not sure. But he's out of office now, too, although not by choice, like me.

I was loved because I told Canadians what they wanted to hear;

because I asked the important questions: "Where's Biafra?" for example. (It's in Nigeria; but before I alerted my fellow citizens, no one even knew.) "Why should I sell your wheat?" I asked our farmers, and how could they not agree? The government has no place in the *farms* of our nation, either. "Get off your asses; get out there and work," I told Vancouver protesters. And from looking at the latest unemployment figures out of British Columbia, it's clear that they didn't listen to me. "*Mangez de la merde*," I told the truck drivers of Montreal, and the public were thrilled; they wanted me to tell off their incompetent postmen, too.

I also pointed out that Members of Parliament are "just nobodies," and nobody could possibly disagree with *that*. And as for the "fuddle duddle" to John Lundrigan, that Tory from Newfoundland, it was probably a phrase which all Canadians have always wanted to say to *all* Tories, but just didn't know how. But, as always, Pierre Elliott Trudeau showed the way.

They called me the magus, the alchemist. In many ways I was; I turned the Canadian dollar into shit. But there were lots of reasons for this, and I have no doubt that lesser mortals would have done the same, but with less finesse, less de Gaullic charm, less wit, less intelligence. *Mon Dieu*, with far less intelligence.

Joseph Phillippe Pierre Yves Elliott Trudeau was born on October 18, 1919, in Montreal. Oh, *pardon moi* — I drifted back into describing myself in the third person, as I often do. The Royal We was hard enough to shake, but dropping the third person was nigh on impossible! But nothing is really impossible for a man like *moi*.

My father, Charles-Emile Trudeau, launched a gas station in 1921, selling it for $1.4 million to Imperial Oil a little over a decade later. This taught me the importance of my inheritance, and it was a lesson which I never forgot. My beloved mother, Grace Elliott Trudeau, had a profound influence on me, until she passed away. I lost contact with her after that, unlike a previous Liberal Prime Minister. I spoke English to my mother, and French to my father, which taught me the relevancy of bilingualism, which I could hardly wait to put into practice.

From the age of 13 until the age of 20, I attended Jesuit schools, where I learned to become perfect through discipline of will. "Reason before passion" was my credo, and I have stayed with it throughout my long and successful life. "O Reason not the need!" cried King Lear, but just look how *he* ended up. *Au contraire*, reason is *all*, and I've tried to rein-in unhealthy passions for the less important things in life: economics, unemployment, Margaret, inflation, friends, the Canadian West.

I was one of the student leaders who fought against conscription in the Second World War, so while others were getting themselves foolishly slaughtered, I was getting an excellent grounding in scholarship: Harvard. The Sorbonne. The London School of Economics. I never did understand the latter.

I took off a number of years and hiked around the world. I figured that I should know the place before I started saving it. I hiked through occupied Germany and Austria. I used phony documents to enter Poland, Hungary and Yugoslavia, where I was jailed for having a fake visa. I visited Turkey, and then Palestine, where I was seized as an Israeli spy by Arabs. From studying all these various political systems, I got the background I would need to declare the *War Measures Act*. And they just watched me, too.

I visited Afghanistan, Pakistan, India and Burma. And then, a series of strange coincidences: I was in Viet Nam a few years before the French were thrown out; I was in China just before the Communists took over; I was in Shanghai shortly before that great city fell to the Reds. I've always been surprised that so many places I've visited have fallen apart shortly after I was there. *Ahh, c'est la guerre.* (Shrug)

Oh, I fought against Duplessis during the Asbestos Strike, and I wrote for *Cité libre*. But my first political beginnings took place when I called the Liberals "idiots" for accepting a nuclear program in Canada. How fortunate for the idiots to have one of the Three Wise Men to come to their rescue and show them the Right Way. Or rather, the Left Way.

In 1965, I landed the first job I ever had: I was elected a Liberal Member of Parliament. I was actually a Socialist at the time, but they never get into power, so I went with the idiots. By 1966, I was Parliamentary Secretary to Mike Pearson. And we all know how important a job like that can be, right Couttsie?

In 1967, I was a most innovative Justice Minister, modernizing a Criminal Code that was so ancient and outmoded, it was criminal.

Everyone agreed with me about the state having no business in our bedrooms. But years later, when my wife made a business about the state of *her* bedrooms, I felt that it had gone a bit too far. But *c'est l'amour.* (Shrug)

My coronation, back in 1968, has been written about so much, I don't even feel it's worth discussing. But how interesting it is, that *not a single one* of the men who ran against me for the Liberal leadership amounted to very much at all. Especially if he got only 195 votes. During the federal election, I managed to bring sex out of the bedroom and into Canadian politics, where it had never been, but where it belongs. Trudeaumania, they called it, and there was no cure for the disease. They were wild about me in '68, they were wild about me in 1974, and they were wild about me in 1980. True, they were only thrilled with me in 1972, and made a near-fatal error in 1979, but only the Pope is infallible. (Shrug)

I danced the frug. I kissed young women, as well as babies. I combed my hair Roman style, wore pastel shirts and Trilby hats. I stripped down to my bathing suit, and showed them how I could live. Although the guy who really took the dive was poor Bob Stanfield.

Some people still bitch about the *War Measures Act* of 1970, as if taking away the civil liberties of twenty million Canadians is such a goddam big thing. But there was an insurrection! The same bleeding hearts love to quote my answer to that TV reporter, Tim Ralfe, when he pressed me about how far I'd go during the FLQ crisis. "Just watch me," I replied. But don't look at me — look at Ralfe! The bugger went on to become the Director of Communications for Joe Clark. It just goes to show you, doesn't it?

But who cares about something as minor as the *War Measures Act*? Why not look at what I and my fellow Liberals accomplished during my 15 years in power: I was a canoeist. I was an outdoorsman. I skied around the world. I spoke with every leader of the world, and outlasted them all. I found jobs for dozens — nay, hundreds — of worthy Liberals, on government boards, government agencies, in the Senate. And isn't finding jobs one of the prime duties of a political leader?

I also dated Barbra Streisand. And Liona Boyd. And Margot Kidder. And no other Prime Minister, President or dictator on this earth can make that statement. I was even married, briefly, if I recall correctly.

Were there any low points in my record-breaking time in office? I cannot deny that unemployment went up slightly in Canada, from 4.5% to 11.2%, and that the inflation rate did increase a tiny bit, from 1.5% in late 1970 to 12.9% in the summer of 1981, and the federal deficit nudged up from $576 million in 1968-69 to around $30 billion, when I left office in early 1984. But look on the bright side: inflation was far, far worse in Argentina and Israel.

I called for a Just Society, and that's all that was left when I was done with it. And although some have suggested that I chose Cabinet Ministers like I chose wives — don't they realize that I was forced to choose from elected MPs? — and that I misunderstood the West — what's to understand? The vast majority of Canadians are well aware that I single-handedly, saved Canada from falling apart, by successfully defeating the Quebec Referendum in 1980, and bringing back the Canadian Constitution, shortly after.

No, I won't stand for all this carping and cavilling, especially now that I am out of office. It was clear from the start that the free market wouldn't work, and has not our economy proven that? (Shrug)

Politics is such a thankless profession! You give a finger, and they take a Salmon Arm. The Canadian people went through over 15 years of near-flawless leadership and governing, and all they do is bitch, just like the ancient Israelites complaining to Moses after leaving Egypt. Exactly like that, in fact.

But it's not my fault if we haven't reached the promised land in Canada, in spite of my inspired leadership. If you people aren't willing to get off your asses and find jobs, you get what you deserve. *Mangez de la merde*. You're just nobodies, that's all; just nobodies. Fuddle duddle. I thought I could get you to fly with me, but I couldn't get you off the ground. You turkeys.
IT WAS ALL YOUR FAULT.

shrug

WILLIAM LYON MACKENZIE KING

"The medium is the message." — Marshall McLuhan

Imagine how excited I was to hear, through my medium, that this book was going to be created. Although my diary of 57 years has been published in bits and pieces — and thoroughly misunderstood in such books as *A Very Double Life* — I am delighted to get this chance to set the record straight, even if I have to do it from beyond.

Call me Willie, as my mother's contemporary, and a fellow-author, Mr. Herman Melville, might begin this. I could start with my own birth, in 1874, but like all Great Men, one has to look back a generation or two, to see the real influences on my life. My grandfather, for one — William Lyon Mackenzie, 1795-1861 — was a great publisher, an inspired editor, and a so-so rebel, back in 1837, when he led 750 farmers in a major uprising, just north of Toronto.

My Mother, Isabel Grace Mackenzie, was born in 1843, the 13th child of that great political leader, William Lyon Mackenzie. She was not like other children: She was the brightest, the most beautiful, the most magnificent, the most awesome, the most precious Woman who was ever born on this earth, probably including the Virgin Mary, whose son also did rather well. Isabel Grace — oh, just the writing down of that name sends me into rapture! — had a painful and difficult childhood, for She was mocked and ill-treated, due to Her father's rather strange political career. I have no doubt that all those who made Her childhood an agony were eventually punished, whether through disease, accident (although there are no accidents), lingering death, or having Tories represent them in Parliament, which is really the same thing.

In 1872, Isabel Grace — there's that exquisite name again! — married John King, a lawyer, although no man — even myself — could be worthy of Her. Somehow this Goddess gave birth to four (4) children, so they must have engaged in s—x at least 4 (four) occasions, although I'd like to think that it was no more often than that.

The loving couple settled in Berlin, Ontario, which later changed its name to Kitchener, due to certain minor tensions overseas. My

167

childhood was a tense one, owing to the frequent tellings of my grandfather's tragic life story by my Mother. It was made clear to me that I had a Moral Obligation to Restore the Honour of our Family Name, so besmirched by the exile of Our Rebel Hero.

I was, understandably, a brilliant student, and entered the University of Toronto at the age of 17, where I was soon the assistant editor of the *Varsity*. I was nicknamed "Rex," although I was never quite sure whether this was due to my last name, or in honour of the dog of the editor of *Varsity*.

I studied hard at U. of T., and led the normal life of a typical young student in the 1890s: studying, reading, attending classes, and saving ruined women from the depths of depravity.

After graduating from university in 1895, I wrote for The Toronto *Globe*, known at that time as "Toronto's local paper." Within a year, I had completed my Honours BA, earned my law degree, and had a year's experience as a journalist. Many of the women, by that time, had returned to the streets, but that is another matter.

I was a most impressive journalist, writing fierce exposés of cheap labour in Toronto. The ruined women weren't that cheap, now that I think of it. I then went off and studied at Harvard, with a half-dozen pictures of Mother on my walls, to keep me on the straight and narrow.

While continuing my studies in England, the Laurier administration offered me a position as deputy minister in the newly-formed Department of Labour, and the editorship of a new publication, *Labour Gazette*. Wilfie had just been elected to his second term as Prime Minister, so I quickly returned home, partly to fill this exciting new position, and mainly because I wished to be close to Mother. If you had known Her, you would have felt the same way.

In 1901, I told my Mother what every mother wants to hear from her son: I whispered to her, "If I ever do become Prime Minister, or come near to such a mark, it will be due to your life and love that I have done so." She embraced me, and I didn't wash where She touched me until other civil servants began to complain.

For the next seven years, I worked long hours in gloomy Ottawa, which, I gather, hasn't changed much. I became known as a labour trouble-shooter, unlike some of the company owners, who used to shoot labour. I am proud of my accomplishments, such as the agreement I negotiated with the Imperial Japanese government for the Canadian government, which severely limited Japanese immigration to Canada. I also managed to exclude immigration from India as well. Since the native Canadian Indians were already here, it was impossible to limit them from coming, dammit.

I was a hit!! The Toronto *Globe* raved about "the brilliant young administrator" in Ottawa in 1908, and they were talking about me! I was seen as a friend of labour, so when I was elected to Parliament at the age of 33, and was Minister of Labour from 1908 to 1910, no one was suprised. Certainly not my beloved, blessed Mother. As I thought at the time, there was a reward in this for Her, as well as for me; reward for the sacrifices that Her father, William Lyon Mackenzie, made. (In 1912, I managed to prevent an unsympathetic biography of my grandfather from being published; power is a wonderful thing, as I was quickly learning).

In 1911, a dreadful thing occurred, but it was one of those nasty, unpleasant things that can only happen in a democracy: Laurier and I went down to defeat, and the wretched Tories, lead by Robert Laird Borden took over.

But things soon picked up. In 1914, when that skirmish over in Europe was beginning, I was asked to head the Rockefeller Foundation's new Department of Industrial Relations. Suddenly, I had the support, trust and friendship of one of the richest and most powerful men in the world, John D. Rockefeller! It was like being buddies with Sir Wilfrid Laurier, except this guy had money.

By the end of the Great War, I had a dreadful few years: My father died. My sister died. My brother was dying. And my Mother and I lost contact for awhile owing to her passing from this plane to beyond. And Laurier and I lost another election.

Then, as fate would have it, Wilfrid Laurier died, in February, 1919. And in August of the same year, I was chosen the leader of the federal Liberal party! Oh, Mother! If only You could have been there in body as you were in spirit! Mother, destiny had intended me to continue to carry on the fight which Grandfather commenced so bravely on behalf of the common people in their struggle.

And struggle we did. In 1920, Borden was replaced by Arthur Meighen, the author of that stupid 1917 Conscription Bill which drove the French-Canadians to apoplexy. So I knew exactly what

to do, in the 1921 election: nothing. I figured that if I never out-
lined a clear and intelligible policy in my election campaign, I'd
irritate nobody. And this inspired concept of non-leadership has
worked wondrously well for the federal Grits, right to this day. Well,
at least until 1984, which was after my time, anyway.

Well, it finally happened: on December 29, 1921, the grandson
of the rebel took office as the Prime Minister of Canada — and
without a single shot fired. It was a narrow majority government,
however, so I continued in my policy and gave my people nothing.
When I went to the people in October of 1925, there was nothing
for the rotten Tories to attack!

It didn't work. And H.G. Wells' *The Invisible Man* had been such
a big best-seller, too. The voters elected 116 Tories, 99 Liberals,
24 Progressives, and 6 Independents — the fools. Not only that, I
had lost my seat, which made it tough to try and get the Speaker's
attention during Question Period.

But hell hath no fury like a King scorned, to coin a phrase. I
brilliantly recovered a Parliamentary majority, defeated the Evil
Conservatives, and managed to kick out my hated enemy, Arthur
Meighen.

It's never really been told before, but here's what I did: I told
the Governor General, Lord Byng, that I would carry on as P.M.,
with the support of the Progressives, who didn't much believe in
doing anything in government, either. Byng, the rotter, told me that
I should resign. So I asked him for a dissolution of Parliament, and
he refused me again. So I quickly resigned, was replaced by
Meighen, who tripped up within 72 hours, and was defeated by
a single vote!

Anyway, the voters went to the polls that fall, for the second time
in a year. Mother was with me, in the campaign, voting as often
as She could (It's an old Liberal tradition). And the God of our fathers
had chosen me — as he did King Saul, for the ancient Hebrews.
From then on, I was to go forward in the strength of God, with his
Might and Right, to battle as my forefathers had battled, for the
right of the People, and do God's will on earth, even as it is done
in Heaven. God, I finally realized, was a True Grit.

As the world knows, we won a majority government. Meighen
was defeated and he resigned, replaced by Richard Bennett, a lawyer

with almost as much money as Rockefeller, but less power, thank God.

People made fun of me, since I was a bachelor, and in my 50s, but they never knew what a rich and vibrant private life I had with my dogs and with Mother. We used to have long conversations — in fact some of my best ideas came from Mother and the dogs.

I had inherited Laurier's house in Ottawa, where I lived until my passing. But I spent my summers up at Kingsmere, my country estate just a few miles outside Ottawa. I had lots of sheep, and used to collect the ruins of historical buildings which had fallen into disarray under the rule of the Tories.

No, I never did find a woman who was right for me. For one thing, she would have to possess all the qualities which I demanded in a wife: she had to be born in 1843. She had to be named Isabel Grace. She had to be the daughter of a great Canadian politician and rebel leader. In a nutshell, she had to be my Mother. As you can well imagine, this limited my dating options greatly. And speaking of Mom, which I frequently did and still do, little did Canadians of the 20s, 30s, and 40s know, when they asked for guidance from above, that they were getting it on a regular basis.

Things sort of fell apart in 1929, with the Great Depression, as it came to be known. I think I blew it, when I announced that "I would not give a five cent piece to any Conservative provincial party which had opposed me." How was I to know how many people could have used a nickel, in those days? So the Canadian people elected a Conservative government in the summer of 1930 — they're only human, you know — and they had to suffer under the incompetent leadership of R.B. Bennett.

In 1932, in the worst depths of the Depression, I had some of my best times. I spoke to Mother regularly, and Sir Wilfrid Laurier gave me some great advice, as well. Now, it is an honoured tradition for political leaders to discuss matters with their predecessors, but what made this so special was the fact that Laurier had been dead for over a dozen years. What he told me was most profound: that I would lead our party to a majestic victory in the next election.

My slogan in 1935 was superb: KING OR CHAOS. It had a nice ring to it, and although most Canadians didn't know what it meant, you can't argue with a great idea, when it comes from the dead.

171

The late 30s were wonderful years, since I celebrated the centenary of the Mackenzie rebellion in 1937, and visited the Third Reich. What a great time I had there! The Fuehrer was a charming fellow. I told him that we had a lot in common. After all, Berlin was my hometown, too! He liked that. I told him that I wasn't too hot for Jews either. He liked that, too. Then I told him that I had no intention whatsoever of taking any of his Jews off his hands, and he was a bit put off.

He deeply impressed me with the great highways he was building, and the way he created such fine discipline in his country. Why, he had almost single-handedly eliminated unemployment, just by throwing Jews and Communists out of work! I told him it was a great idea, but we just didn't have enough of both in Canada to make it work. What a character he was! It's true, he finally threw Europe into some disarray, but I sure liked him a lot better than Mitch Hepburn, back in Ontario.

By 1940, when my old chum Adolf was busy on the other side of the Atlantic, I was re-elected with an overwhelming majority: 181 Liberals to 40 Conservatives and 8 CCFers. Once again, I didn't have to do much at all. I merely hired C.D. Howe as Minister of Everything On Earth, and I sat back, relaxed, talked to Mom, played with Pat I, II or III, and let the clouds of war roll by.

On April 20, 1948, I surpassed Sir Robert Walpole's record of leadership: 7,619 days in office. I felt that it was time for me to finally think about stepping down. But when to do it? Timing is everything! I finally decided on three days in August on which to hold the Liberal convention, since the stars were perfect, on the 5th, 6th and 7th of that month. I don't know why others can't see the importance of these things.

I made sure that Uncle Louis would replace me; I felt that it was time for another one of them. After all, they helped found Canada too, you know. It was over a quarter-century since the Liberals had had a new leader, and it must have been quite a blow for them, but they clearly survived.

I had done a masterful job, if I say so myself. I regarded my having helped to keep Canada united throughout the war as the main contribution I had made, although making the Liberals the true Ruling Party of Canada was probably the other.

I wasn't too upset about dying, I must admit. After all, I'd been PM for over 21 years, and I got to be buried right next to Mother, which is every man's dream. I was put off; when my 57 years of diaries were found and began to be published; that stuff was for Mother's and Pats' ears alone. Still, I helped save the country, and that makes it all worthwhile. I didn't just do it for myself but for my family. Grandfather? Mother? Is anybody there?